CONFESSION OF ST. PATRICK
AND RELATED TEXTS

INCLUDING

HIS EPISTLE TO THE CHRISTIAN SUBJECTS OF THE TYRANT COROTICUS, ST. FIECH'S METRICAL LIFE OF ST. PATRICK, AND THE TRIPARTITE LIFE OF ST. PATRICK

by

St. Patrick, *et al.*

© 2010 Benediction Classics, Oxford.

Contents

CONFESSION OF ST. PATRICK 1

ST. PATRICK'S EPISTLE TO THE CHRISTIAN
SUBJECTS OF THE TYRANT COROTICUS 17

ST. FIECH'S METRICAL LIFE OF ST. PATRICK 23

TRIPARTITE LIFE OF ST. PATRICK 31
   PART I. 31
   PART II. 45
   PART III. 73

CONFESSION OF ST. PATRICK

1. I, Patrick, a sinner, a most simple countryman, the least of all the faithful and most contemptible to many, had for father the deacon Calpurnius, son of the late Potitus, a priest, of the settlement [*vicus*] of Bannavem Taburniae; he had a small villa nearby where I was taken captive. I was at that time about sixteen years of age. I did not, indeed, know the true God; and I was taken into captivity in Ireland with many thousands of people, according to our deserts, for quite drawn away from God, we did not keep his precepts, nor were we obedient to our priests who used to remind us of our salvation. And the Lord brought down on us the fury of his being and scattered us among many nations, even to the ends of the earth, where I, in my smallness, am now to be found among foreigners.

2. And there the Lord opened my mind to an awareness of my unbelief, in order that, even so late, I might remember my transgressions and turn with all my heart to the Lord my God, who had regard for my insignificance and pitied my youth and ignorance. And he watched over me before I knew him, and before I learned sense or even distinguished between good and evil, and he protected me, and consoled me as a father would his son.

3. Therefore, indeed, I cannot keep silent, nor would it be proper, so many favours and graces has the Lord deigned to bestow on me in the land of my captivity. For after chastisement from God, and recognizing him, our way to repay him is to exalt him and confess his wonders before every nation under heaven.

4. For there is no other God, nor ever was before, nor shall be hereafter, but God the Father, unbegotten and without beginning, in whom all things began, whose are all things, as we have been taught; and his son Jesus Christ, who manifestly always existed with the Father, before the beginning of time in the spirit with the Father, indescribably begotten before all things, and all things visible and invisible were made by him. He was made man, conquered death and was received into Heaven, to the Father who gave him all power over every name in Heaven and on Earth and in Hell, so that every tongue should confess that Jesus Christ is Lord and God, in whom we believe. And we look to his imminent coming again, the judge of the living and the dead, who will render to each according to his deeds. And he poured out his Holy Spirit on us in abundance, the gift and pledge of immortality, which makes the believers and the obedient into sons of God and coheirs of Christ who is revealed, and we worship one God in the Trinity of holy name.

5. He himself said through the prophet: 'Call upon me in the day of' trouble; I will deliver you, and you shall glorify me.' And again: 'It is right to reveal and publish abroad the works of God.'

6. I am imperfect in many things; nevertheless I want my brethren and kinsfolk to know my nature so that they may be able to perceive my soul's desire.

7. I am not ignorant of what is said of my Lord in the Psalm: 'You destroy those who speak a lie.' And again: 'A lying mouth deals death to the soul.' And likewise the Lord says in the Gospel: 'On the day of judgment men shall render account for every idle word they utter.'

8. So it is that I should mightily fear, with terror and trembling, this judgment on the day when no one shall be able to steal away or hide, but each and all shall render account for even our smallest sins before the judgment seat of Christ the Lord.

9. And therefore for some time I have thought of writing, but I have hesitated until now, for truly, I feared to expose myself to the criticism of men, because I have not studied like others, who have assimilated both Law and the Holy Scriptures equally and have never changed their idiom since their infancy, but instead were always learning it in-

creasingly, to perfection, while my idiom and language have been translated into a foreign tongue. So it is easy to prove from a sample of my writing, my ability in rhetoric and the extent of my preparation and knowledge, for as it is said, wisdom shall be recognized in speech, and in understanding, and in knowledge and in the learning of truth.'

10. But why make excuses close to the truth, especially when now I am presuming to try to grasp in my old age what I did not gain in my youth because my sins prevented me from making what I had read my own? But who will believe me, even though I should say it again? A young man, almost a beardless boy, I was taken captive before I knew what I should desire and what I should shun. So, consequently, today I feel ashamed and I am mightily afraid to expose my ignorance, because, [not] eloquent, with a small vocabulary, I am unable to explain as the spirit is eager to do and as the soul and the mind indicate.

11. But had it been given to me as to others, in gratitude I should not have kept silent, and if it should appear that I put myself before others, with my ignorance and my slower speech, in truth, it is written: 'The tongue of the stammerers shall speak rapidly and distinctly.' How much harder must we try to attain it, we of whom it is said: 'You are an epistle of Christ in greeting to the ends of the earth . . . written on your hearts, not with ink but with the Spirit of the living God.' And again, the Spirit witnessed that the rustic life was created by the Most High.

12. I am, then, first of all, countryfied, an exile, evidently unlearned, one who is not able to see into the future, but I know for certain, that before I was humbled I was like a stone lying in deep mire, and he that is mighty came and in his mercy raised me up and, indeed, lifted me high up and placed me on top of the wall. And from there I ought to shout out in gratitude to the Lord for his great favours in this world and for ever, that the mind of man cannot measure.

13. Therefore be amazed, you great and small who fear God, and you men of God, eloquent speakers, listen and contemplate. Who was it summoned me, a fool, from the midst of those who appear wise and learned in the law and powerful in rhetoric and in all things? Me, truly wretched in this world, he inspired before others that I could be—if I would—such a one who, with fear and reverence, and faithfully, without complaint, would come to the people to whom the love of Christ

brought me and gave me in my lifetime, if I should be worthy, to serve them truly and with humility.

14. According, therefore, to the measure of one's faith in the Trinity, one should proceed without holding back from danger to make known the gift of God and everlasting consolation, to spread God's name everywhere with confidence and without fear, in order to leave behind, after my death, foundations for my brethren and sons whom I baptized in the Lord in so many thousands.

15. And I was not worthy, nor was I such that the Lord should grant his humble servant this, that after hardships and such great trials, after captivity, after many years, he should give me so much favour in these people, a thing which in the time of my youth I neither hoped for nor imagined.

16. But after I reached Ireland I used to pasture the flock each day and I used to pray many times a day. More and more did the love of God, and my fear of him and faith increase, and my spirit was moved so that in a day [I said] from one up to a hundred prayers, and in the night a like number; besides I used to stay out in the forests and on the mountain and I would wake up before daylight to pray in the snow, in icy coldness, in rain, and I used to feel neither ill nor any slothfulness, because, as I now see, the Spirit was burning in me at that time.

17. And it was there of course that one night in my sleep I heard a voice saying to me: 'You do well to fast: soon you will depart for your home country.' And again, a very short time later, there was a voice prophesying: 'Behold, your ship is ready.' And it was not close by, but, as it happened, two hundred miles away, where I had never been nor knew any person. And shortly thereafter I turned about and fled from the man with whom I had been for six years, and I came, by the power of God who directed my route to advantage (and I was afraid of nothing), until I reached that ship.

18. And on the same day that I arrived, the ship was setting out from the place, and I said that I had the wherewithal to sail with them; and the steersman was displeased and replied in anger, sharply: 'By no means attempt to go with us.' Hearing this I left them to go to the hut where I was staying, and on the way I began to pray, and before the prayer was finished I heard one of them shouting loudly after me:

'Come quickly because the men are calling you.' And immediately I went back to them and they started to say to me: 'Come, because we are admitting you out of good faith; make friendship with us in any way you wish.' (And so, on that day, I refused to suck the breasts of these men from fear of God, but nevertheless I had hopes that they would come to faith in Jesus Christ, because they were barbarians.) And for this I continued with them, and forthwith we put to sea.

19. And after three days we reached land, and for twenty-eight days journeyed through uninhabited country, and the food ran out and hunger overtook them; and one day the steersman began saying: 'Why is it, Christian? You say your God is great and all-powerful; then why can you not pray for us? For we may perish of hunger; it is unlikely indeed that we shall ever see another human being.' In fact, I said to them, confidently: 'Be converted by faith with all your heart to my Lord God, because nothing is impossible for him, so that today he will send food for you on your road, until you be sated, because everywhere he abounds.' And with God's help this came to pass; and behold, a herd of swine appeared on the road before our eyes, and they slew many of them, and remained there for two nights, and the men were full of their meat and well restored, for many of them had fainted and would otherwise have been left half dead by the wayside. And after this they gave the utmost thanks to God, and I was esteemed in their eyes, and from that day they had food abundantly. They discovered wild honey, besides, and they offered a share to me, and one of them said: 'It is a sacrifice.' Thanks be to God, I tasted none of it.

20. The very same night while I was sleeping Satan attacked me violently, as I will remember as long as I shall be in this body; and there fell on top of me, as it were, a huge rock, and not one of my members had any force. But from whence did it come to me, ignorant in the spirit, to call upon Helias'? And meanwhile I saw the sun rising in the sky, and while I was crying out Helias, Helias' with all my might, lo, the brilliance of that sun fell upon me and immediately shook me free of all the weight; and I believe that I was aided by Christ my Lord, and that his Spirit then was crying out for me, and I hope that it will be so in the day of my affliction, just as it says in the Gospel: 'In that hour', the Lord declares, 'it is not you who speaks but the Spirit of your Father speaking in you.'

21. And a second time, after many years, I was taken captive. On the first night I accordingly remained with my captors, but I heard a divine prophecy, saying to me: 'You shall be with them for two months.' So it happened. On the sixtieth night the Lord delivered me from their hands.

22. On the journey he provided us with food and fire and dry weather every day, until on the tenth day we came upon people. As I mentioned above, we had journeyed through an unpopulated country for twenty-eight days, and in fact the night that we came upon people we had no food.

23. And after a few years I was again in Britain with my parents [kinsfolk], and they welcomed me as a son, and asked me, in faith, that after the great tribulations I had endured I should not go anywhere else away from them. And, of course, there, in a vision of the night, I saw a man whose name was Victoricus coming as if from Ireland with innumerable letters, and he gave me one of them, and I read the beginning of the letter: 'The Voice of the Irish'; and as I was reading the beginning of the letter I seemed at that moment to hear the voice of those who were beside the forest of Foclut which is near the western sea, and they were crying as if with one voice: 'We beg you, holy youth, that you shall come and shall walk again among us.' And I was stung intensely in my heart so that I could read no more, and thus I awoke. Thanks be to God, because after so many years the Lord bestowed on them according to their cry.

24. And another night--God knows, I do not, whether within me or beside me— . . . most words + . . . + which I heard and could not understand, except at the end of the speech it was represented thus: 'He who gave his life for you, he it is who speaks within you.' And thus I awoke, joyful.

25. And on a second occasion I saw Him praying within me, and I was as it were, inside my own body, and I heard Him above me--that is, above my inner self. He was praying powerfully with sighs. And in the course of this I was astonished and wondering, and I pondered who it could be who was praying within me. But at the end of the prayer it was revealed to me that it was the Spirit. And so I awoke and remembered the Apostle's words: 'Likewise the Spirit helps us in our weakness; for we know not how to pray as we ought. But the Spirit

Himself intercedes for us with sighs too deep for utterance.' And again: 'The Lord our advocate intercedes for us.'

26. And then I was attacked by a goodly number of my elders, who [brought up] my sins against my arduous episcopate. That day in particular I was mightily upset, and might have fallen here and for ever; but the Lord generously spared me, a convert, and an alien, for his name's sake, and he came powerfully to my assistance in that state of being trampled down. I pray God that it shall not be held against them as a sin that I fell truly into disgrace and scandal.

27. They brought up against me after thirty years an occurrence I had confessed before becoming a deacon. On account of the anxiety in my sorrowful mind, I laid before my close friend what I had perpetrated on a day--nay, rather in one hour--in my boyhood because I was not yet proof against sin. God knows--I do not--whether I was fifteen years old at the time, and I did not then believe in the living God, nor had I believed, since my infancy; but I remained in death and unbelief until I was severely rebuked, and in truth I was humbled every day by hunger and nakedness.

28. On the other hand, I did not proceed to Ireland of my own accord until I was almost giving up, but through this I was corrected by the Lord, and he prepared me so that today I should be what was once far from me, in order that I should have the care of—or rather, I should be concerned for—the salvation of others, when at that time, still, I was only concerned for myself.

29. Therefore, on that day when I was rebuked, as I have just mentioned, I saw in a vision of the night a document before my face, without honour, and meanwhile I heard a divine prophecy, saying to me: 'We have seen with displeasure the face of the chosen one divested of [his good] name.' And he did not say 'You have seen with displeasure', but 'We have seen with displeasure' (as if He included Himself). He said then: 'He who touches you, touches the apple of my eye.'

30. For that reason, I give thanks to him who strengthened me in all things, so that I should not be hindered in my setting out and also in my work which I was taught by Christ my Lord; but more, from that

state of affairs I felt, within me, no little courage, and vindicated my faith before God and man.

31. Hence, therefore, I say boldly that my conscience is clear now and hereafter. God is my witness that I have not lied in these words to you.

32. But rather, I am grieved for my very close friend, that because of him we deserved to hear such a prophecy. The one to whom I entrusted my soul! And I found out from a goodly number of brethren, before the case was made in my defence (in which I did not take part, nor was I in Britain, nor was it pleaded by me), that in my absence he would fight in my behalf. Besides, he told me himself: 'See, the rank of bishop goes to you'--of which I was not worthy. But how did it come to him, shortly afterwards, to disgrace me publicly, in the presence of all, good and bad, because previously, gladly and of his own free will, he pardoned me, as did the Lord, who is greater than all?

33. I have said enough. But all the same, I ought not to conceal God's gift which he lavished on us in the land of my captivity, for then I sought him resolutely, and I found him there, and he preserved me from all evils (as I believe) through the in-dwelling of his Spirit, which works in me to this day. Again, boldly, but God knows, if this had been made known to me by man, I might, perhaps, have kept silent for the love of Christ.

34. Thus I give untiring thanks to God who kept me faithful in the day of my temptation, so that today I may confidently offer my soul as a living sacrifice for Christ my Lord; who am I, Lord? or, rather, what is my calling? that you appeared to me in so great a divine quality, so that today among the barbarians I might constantly exalt and magnify your name in whatever place I should be, and not only in good fortune, but even in affliction? So that whatever befalls me, be it good or bad, I should accept it equally, and give thanks always to God who revealed to me that I might trust in him, implicitly and forever, and who will encourage me so that, ignorant, and in the last days, I may dare to undertake so devout and so wonderful a work; so that I might imitate one of those whom, once, long ago, the Lord already pre-ordained to be heralds of his Gospel to witness to all peoples to the ends of the earth. So are we seeing, and so it is fulfilled; behold, we are witnesses be-

cause the Gospel has been preached as far as the places beyond which no man lives.

35. But it is tedious to describe in detail all my labours one by one. I will tell briefly how most holy God frequently delivered me, from slavery, and from the twelve trials with which my soul was threatened, from man traps as well, and from things I am not able to put into words. I would not cause offence to readers, but I have God as witness who knew all things even before they happened, that, though I was a poor, ignorant waif, still he gave me abundant warnings through divine prophecy.

36. Whence came to me this wisdom which was not my own, I who neither knew the number of days nor had knowledge of God? Whence came the so great and so healthful gift of knowing or rather loving God, though I should lose homeland and family?

37. And many gifts were offered to me with weeping and tears, and I offended them [the donors], and also went against the wishes of a good number of my elders; but guided by God, I neither agreed with them nor deferred to them, not by my own grace but by God who is victorious in me and withstands them all, so that I might come to the Irish people to preach the Gospel and endure insults from unbelievers; that I might hear scandal of my travels, and endure many persecutions to the extent of prison; and so that I might give up my free birthright for the advantage of others, and if I should be worthy, I am ready [to give] even my life without hesitation; and most willingly for His name. And I choose to devote it to him even unto death, if God grant it to me.

38. I am greatly God's debtor, because he granted me so much grace, that through me many people would be reborn in God, and soon a after confirmed, and that clergy would be ordained everywhere for them, the masses lately come to belief, whom the Lord drew from the ends of the earth, just as he once promised through his prophets: 'To you shall the nations come from the ends of the earth, and shall say, "Our fathers have inherited naught but lies, worthless things in which there is no profit."' And again: 'I have set you to be a light for the Gentiles that you may bring salvation to the uttermost ends of the earth.'

39. And I wish to wait then for his promise which is never unfulfilled, just as it is promised in the Gospel: 'Many shall come from east

and west and shall sit at table with Abraham and Isaac and Jacob.' Just as we believe that believers will come from all the world,

40. So for that reason one should, in fact, fish well and diligently, just as the Lord foretells and teaches, saying, 'Follow me, and I will make you fishers of men,' and, again, through the prophets: "Behold, I am sending forth many fishers and hunters," says the Lord,' et cetera. So it behoved us to spread our nets, that a vast multitude and throng might be caught for God, and so there might be clergy everywhere who baptized and exhorted a needy and desirous people. Just as the Lord says in the Gospel, admonishing and instructing: 'Go therefore and make disciples of all nations, baptizing them in the name of the Father and of the Son and of the Holy Spirit, teaching them to observe all that I have commanded you; and lo, I am with you always to the end of time.' And again he says: 'Go forth into the world and preach the Gospel to all creation. He who believes and is baptized shall be saved; but he who does not believe shall be condemned.' And again: 'This Gospel of the Kingdom shall be preached throughout the whole world as a witness to all nations; and then the end of the world shall come.' And likewise the Lord foretells through the prophet: 'And it shall come to pass in the last days (sayeth the Lord) that I will pour out my spirit upon all flesh, and your sons and daughters shall prophesy, and your young men shall see visions and your old men shall dream dreams; yea, and on my menservants and my maidservants in those days I will pour out my Spirit and they shall prophesy.' And in Hosea he says: 'Those who are not my people I will call my people, and those not beloved I will call my beloved, and in the very place where it was said to them, "You are not my people," they will be called "Sons of the living God."'

41. So, how is it that in Ireland, where they never had any knowledge of God but, always, until now, cherished idols and unclean things, they are lately become a people of the Lord, and are called children of God; the sons of the Irish [*Scotti*] and the daughters of the chieftains are to be seen as monks and virgins of Christ.

42. And there was, besides, a most beautiful, blessed, native-born noble Irish [*Scotta*] woman of adult age whom I baptized; and a few days later she had reason to come to us to intimate that she had received a prophecy from a divine messenger [who] advised her that she should become a virgin of Christ and she would draw nearer to God.

Thanks be to God, six days from then, opportunely and most eagerly, she took the course that all virgins of God take, not with their fathers' consent but enduring the persecutions and deceitful hindrances of their parents. Notwithstanding that, their number increases, (we do not know the number of them that are so reborn) besides the widows, and those who practise self-denial. Those who are kept in slavery suffer the most. They endure terrors and constant threats, but the Lord has given grace to many of his handmaidens, for even though they are forbidden to do so, still they resolutely follow his example.

43. So it is that even if I should wish to separate from them in order to go to Britain, and most willingly was I prepared to go to my homeland and kinsfolk—and not only there, but as far as Gaul to visit the brethren there, so that I might see the faces of the holy ones of my Lord, God knows how strongly I desired this—I am bound by the Spirit, who witnessed to me that if I did so he would mark me out as guilty, and I fear to waste the labour that I began, and not I, but Christ the Lord, who commanded me to come to be with them for the rest of my life, if the Lord shall will it and shield me from every evil, so that I may not sin before him.

44. So I hope that I did as I ought, but I do not trust myself as long as I am in this mortal body, for he is strong who strives daily to turn me away from the faith and true holiness to which I aspire until the end of my life for Christ my Lord, but the hostile flesh is always dragging one down to death, that is, to unlawful attractions. And I know in part why I did not lead a perfect life like other believers, but I confess to my Lord and do not blush in his sight, because I am not lying; from the time when I came to know him in my youth, the love of God and fear of him increased in me, and right up until now, by God's favour, I have kept the faith.

45. What is more, let anyone laugh and taunt if he so wishes. I am not keeping silent, nor am I hiding the signs and wonders that were shown to me by the Lord many years before they happened, [he] who knew everything, even before the beginning of time.

46. Thus, I should give thanks unceasingly to God, who frequently forgave my folly and my negligence, in more than one instance so as not to be violently angry with me, who am placed as his helper, and I did not easily assent to what had been revealed to me, as the Spirit was

urging; and the Lord took pity on me thousands upon thousands of times, because he saw within me that I was prepared, but that I was ignorant of what to do in view of my situation; because many were trying to prevent this mission. They were talking among themselves behind my back, and saying: 'Why is this fellow throwing himself into danger among enemies who know not God?' Not from malice, but having no liking for it; likewise, as I myself can testify, they perceived my rusticity. And I was not quick to recognize the grace that was then in me; I now know that I should have done so earlier.

47. Now I have put it frankly to my brethren and co-workers, who have believed me because of what I have foretold and still foretell to strengthen and reinforce your faith. I wish only that you, too, would make greater and better efforts. This will be my pride, for 'a wise son makes a proud father'.

48. You know, as God does, how I went about among you from my youth in the faith of truth and in sincerity of heart. As well as to the heathen among whom I live, I have shown them trust and always show them trust. God knows I did not cheat any one of them, nor consider it, for the sake of God and his Church, lest I arouse them and [bring about] persecution for them and for all of us, and lest the Lord's name be blasphemed because of me, for it is written: 'Woe to the men through whom the name of the Lord is blasphemed.'

49. For even though I am ignorant in all things, nevertheless I attempted to safeguard some and myself also. And I gave back again to my Christian brethren and the virgins of Christ and the holy women the small unasked for gifts that they used to give me or some of their ornaments which they used to throw on the altar. And they would be offended with me because I did this. But in the hope of eternity, I safeguarded myself carefully in all things, so that they might not cheat me of my office of service on any pretext of dishonesty, and so that I should not in the smallest way provide any occasion for defamation or disparagement on the part of unbelievers.

50. What is more, when I baptized so many thousands of people, did I hope for even half a jot from any of them? [If so] Tell me, and I will give it back to you. And when the Lord ordained clergy everywhere by my humble means, and I freely conferred office on them, if I asked

any of them anywhere even for the price of one shoe, say so to my face and I will give it back.

51. More, I spent for you so that they would receive me. And I went about among you, and everywhere for your sake, in danger, and as far as the outermost regions beyond which no one lived, and where no one had ever penetrated before, to baptize or to ordain clergy or to confirm people. Conscientiously and gladly I did all this work by God's gift for your salvation.

52. From time to time I gave rewards to the kings, as well as making payments to their sons who travel with me; notwithstanding which, they seized me with my companions, and that day most avidly desired to kill me. But my time had not yet come. They plundered everything they found on us anyway, and fettered me in irons; and on the fourteenth day the Lord freed me from their power, and whatever they had of ours was given back to us for the sake of God on account of the indispensable friends whom we had made before.

53. Also you know from experience how much I was paying to those who were administering justice in all the regions, which I visited often. I estimate truly that I distributed to them not less than the price of fifteen men, in order that you should enjoy my company and I enjoy yours, always, in God. I do not regret this nor do I regard it as enough. I am paying out still and I shall pay out more. The Lord has the power to grant me that I may soon spend my own self, for your souls.

54. Behold, I call on God as my witness upon my soul that I am not lying; nor would I write to you for it to be an occasion for flattery or selfishness, nor hoping for honour from any one of you. Sufficient is the honour which is not yet seen, but in which the heart has confidence. He who made the promise is faithful; he never lies.

55. But I see that even here and now, I have been exalted beyond measure by the Lord, and I was not worthy that he should grant me this, while I know most certainly that poverty and failure suit me better than wealth and delight (but Christ the Lord was poor for our sakes; I certainly am wretched and unfortunate; even if I wanted wealth I have no resources, nor is it my own estimation of myself, for daily I expect to be murdered or betrayed or reduced to slavery if the occasion arises. But I fear nothing, because of the promises of Heaven; for I have cast

myself into the hands of Almighty God, who reigns everywhere. As the prophet says: 'Cast your burden on the Lord and he will sustain you.'

56. Behold now I commend my soul to God who is most faithful and for whom I perform my mission in obscurity, but he is no respecter of persons and he chose me for this service that I might be one of the least of his ministers.

57. For which reason I should make return for all that he returns me. But what should I say, or what should I promise to my Lord, for I, alone, can do nothing unless he himself vouchsafe it to me. But let him search my heart and [my] nature, for I crave enough for it, even too much, and I am ready for him to grant me that I drink of his chalice, as he has granted to others who love him.

58. Therefore may it never befall me to be separated by my God from his people whom he has won in this most remote land. I pray God that he gives me perseverance, and that he will deign that I should be a faithful witness for his sake right up to the time of my passing.

59. And if at any time I managed anything of good for the sake of my God whom I love, I beg of him that he grant it to me to shed my blood for his name with proselytes and captives, even should I be left unburied, or even were my wretched body to be torn limb from limb by dogs or savage beasts, or were it to be devoured by the birds of the air, I think, most surely, were this to have happened to me, I had saved both my soul and my body. For beyond any doubt on that day we shall rise again in the brightness of the sun, that is, in the glory of Christ Jesus our Redeemer, as children of the living God and co-heirs of Christ, made in his image; for we shall reign through him and for him and in him.

60. For the sun we see rises each day for us at [his] command, but it will never reign, neither will its splendour last, but all who worship it will come wretchedly to punishment. We, on the other hand, shall not die, who believe in and worship the true sun, Christ, who will never die, no more shall he die who has done Christ's will, but will abide for ever just as Christ abides for ever, who reigns with God the Father Almighty and with the Holy Spirit before the beginning of time and now and for ever and ever. Amen.

61. Behold over and over again I would briefly set out the words of my confession. I testify in truthfulness and gladness of heart before God and his holy angels that I never had any reason, except the Gospel and his promises, ever to have returned to that nation from which I had previously escaped with difficulty.

62. But I entreat those who believe in and fear God, whoever deigns to examine or receive this document composed by the obviously unlearned sinner Patrick in Ireland, that nobody shall ever ascribe to my ignorance any trivial thing that I achieved or may have expounded that was pleasing to God, but accept and truly believe that it would have been the gift of God. And this is my confession before I die.

ST. PATRICK'S EPISTLE TO THE CHRISTIAN SUBJECTS OF THE TYRANT COROTICUS

I, Patrick, a sinner and unlearned, have been appointed a bishop in Ireland, and I accept from God what I am. I dwell amongst barbarians as a proselyte and a fugitive for the love of God. He will testify that it is so. It is not my wish to pour forth so many harsh and severe things; but I am forced by zeal for God and the truth of Christ, who raised me up for my neighbors and sons, for whom I have forsaken my country and parents, and would give up even life itself, if I were worthy. I have vowed to my God to teach these people, though I should be despised by them, to whom I have written with my own hand to be given to the soldiers to be sent to Coroticus—I do not say to my fellow-citizens, nor to the fellow-citizens of pious Romans, but to the fellow-citizens of the devil, through their evil deeds and hostile practices. They live in death, companions of the apostate Scots and Picts, blood-thirsty men, ever ready to redden themselves with the blood of innocent Christians, numbers of whom I have begotten to God and confirmed in Christ.

On the day following that in which they were clothed in white and received the chrism of neophytes, they were cruelly cut up and slain with the sword by the above mentioned; and I sent a letter by a holy priest, whom I have taught from his infancy, with some clerics,

Epistle to the Subjects of Coroticus

begging that they would restore some of the plunder or the baptized captives; but they laughed at them. Therefore I know not whether I should grieve most for those who were slain, or for those whom the devil insnared into the eternal pains of hell, where they will be chained like him. For whoever commits sin is the slave of sin, and is called the son of the devil.

Wherefore let every man know who fears God that they are estranged from me, and from Christ my God, whose ambassador I am—these patricides, fratricides, and ravening wolves, who devour the people of the Lord as if they were bread; as it is said: "The wicked have dissipated thy law," wherein in these latter times Ireland has been well and prosperously planted and instructed. Thanks be to God, I usurp nothing; I share with these whom He hath called and predestinated to preach the Gospel in much persecution, even to the ends of the earth. But the enemy hath acted invidiously towards me through the tyrant Coroticus, who fears neither God nor His priests whom He hath chosen, and committed to them the high, divine power: "Whomsoever they shall bind on earth shall be bound in heaven."

I beseech you, therefore, who are the holy ones of God and humble of heart, that you will not be flattered by them, and that you will neither eat nor drink with them, nor receive their alms, until they do penance with many tears, and liberate the servants of God and the baptized hand-maids of Christ, for whom he was crucified and died. "He that offereth sacrifice of the goods of the poor, is as one that sacrificeth the son in the presence of the father." "Riches, he saith, which the unjust accumulate shall be vomited forth from his belly, the angel of death shall drag him away, he shall be punished with the fury of dragons, the tongue of the adder shall slay him, inextinguishable fire shall consume him." Hence, "Woe to those who fill themselves with things which are not their own." And "what doth it profit a man if he gain the whole world and suffer the loss of his soul?" It were too long to discuss one by one, or to select from the law, testimonies against such cupidity. Avarice is a mortal sin. "Thou shall not covet thy neighbor's goods." "Thou shall not kill." The homicide cannot dwell with Christ. "He who hateth his brother is a murderer," and "and he who loveth not his brother abideth in death." How much more guilty is he who hath defiled his hands with the blood of the sons of God, whom He hath recently acquired in the ends of the earth by our humble exhortations!

Did I come to Ireland according to God or according to the flesh? Who compelled me? I was led by the Spirit, that I should see my relatives no more. Have I not a pious mercy towards that nation which formerly took me captive? According to the flesh, I am of noble birth, my father being a Decurio. I do not regret or blush for having bartered my nobility for the good of others. I am a servant in Christ unto a foreign people for the ineffable glory of eternal life, which is in Christ Jesus my Lord; though my own people do not acknowledge me: "A prophet is without honor in his own country." Are we not from one stock, and have we not one God for our Father? As He has said: "He that is not with me is against me, and he that gathereth not with me scattereth." Is it not agreed that one pulleth down and another buildeth? I seek not my own.

Not to me be praise, but to God, who hath put into my heart this desire that I should be one of the hunters and fishers whom, of old, God hath announced should appear in the last days. I am reviled—what shall I do, O Lord? I am greatly despised. Lo! thy sheep are torn around me, and plundered by the above-mentioned robbers, aided by the soldiers of Coroticus: the betrayers of Christians into the hands of the Picts and Scots are far from the charity of God. Ravening wolves have scattered the flock of the Lord, which, with the greatest diligence, was increasing in Ireland; the sons of the Irish and the daughters of kings who are monks and virgins of Christ are too many to enumerate. Therefore the oppression of the great is not pleasing to thee now, and never shall be.

Who of the saints would not dread to share in the feasts or amusements of such persons? They fill their houses with the spoils of the Christian dead, they live by rapine, they know not the poison, the deadly food, which they present to their friends and children; as Eve did not understand that she offered death to her husband, so are all those who work evil: they labor to work out death and eternal punishment.

It is the custom of the Christians of Rome and Gaul to send holy men to the Franks and other nations, with many thousand solidi, to redeem baptized captives. You who slay them, and sell them to foreign nations ignorant of God, deliver the members of Christ, as it were, into a den of wolves. What hope have you in God? Whoever agrees with you, or commands you, God will judge him. I know not what I can say, or what I can speak more of the departed sons of God slain cruelly by the sword. It is written: "Weep with them that weep." And again: "If any member suffers anything, all the members suffer with it." Therefore the Church laments and bewails her sons and daughters, not slain by the sword, but sent away to distant countries,

Epistle to the Subjects of Coroticus

where sin is more shameless and abounds. There free-born Christian men are sold and enslaved amongst the wicked, abandoned, and apostate Picts.

Therefore I cry out with grief and sorrow. O beautiful and well-beloved brethren and children! whom I have brought forth in Christ in such multitudes, what shall I do for you? I am not worthy before God or man to come to your assistance. The wicked have prevailed over us. We have become outcasts. It would seem that they do not think we have one baptism and one Father, God. They think it an indignity that we have been born in Ireland; as He said: "Have ye not one God? Why do ye each forsake his neighbor?" Therefore I grieve for you—I grieve, O my beloved ones! But, on the other hand, I congratulate myself I have not labored for nothing—my journey has not been in vain. This horrible and amazing crime has been permitted to take place. Thanks be to God, ye who have believed and have been baptized have gone from earth to paradise. Certainly, ye have begun to migrate where there is no night or death or sorrow; but ye shall exult like young bulls loosed from their bonds and tread down the wicked under your feet as dust.

Truly, you shall reign with the apostles and prophets and martyrs, and obtain the eternal kingdom, as He hath testified, saying: "They shall come from the east and the west, and shall sit down with Abraham and Isaac and Jacob in the kingdom of heaven." Without are dogs, and sorcerers, and murderers, and liars, and perjurers, and they shall have their part in the everlasting lake of fire. Nor does the apostle say without reason: "If the just are scarcely saved, where shall the sinner, the impious, and the transgressor of the law appear?" Where will Coroticus and his wicked rebels against Christ find themselves when they shall see rewards distributed amongst the baptized women? What will he think of his miserable kingdom, which shall pass away in a moment, like clouds or smoke, which are dispersed by the wind? So shall deceitful sinners perish before the face of the Lord, and the just shall feast with great confidence with Christ, and judge the nations, and rule over unjust kings, for ever and ever. Amen.

I testify before God and His angels that it shall be so, as He hath intimated to my ignorance. These are not my words that I have set forth in Latin, but those of God and the prophets and apostles, who never lied: "He that believeth shall be saved, but he that believeth not shall be condemned."

God hath said it. I entreat whosoever is a servant of God that he be a willing bearer of this letter, that he be not drawn aside by any one, but that he shall see it read before all the people in the presence of Coroticus himself, that, if God inspire them, they may some time return to God, and repent, though late; that they may liberate the baptized captives, and repent for their homicides of the Lord's brethren; so that they may deserve of God to live and to be whole here and hereafter. The peace of the Father, and of the Son, and of the Holy Ghost. Amen.

ST. FIECH'S METRICAL LIFE OF ST. PATRICK

*Written in the Irish Language
about 1,400 years ago.*

I.

At Nemthur Saint Patrick was born,
    As history handed it down;
And when but sixteen years of age,
    A captive was led from that town.

II.

Siccoth was Saint Patrick's first name;
    His father Calphurn without miss;
His grandfather Otide was styled;
    He was nephew of Deacon Odisse.

III.

Six years did he live in dark bonds,
    And the food of the Gentile ate not;
And Cathraige by men he was called,
    Since to work for four homes was his lot.

IV.

To the servant of Milcho 'twas said
    To pass o'er the seas and the plain;
Then stood angel Victor on rock,
    And his footprints to this day remain.

V.

Departed Saint Patrick o'er Alps –
    On his way all successful he hies;
And with German remained in the South
    'Neath Letavia's wide-spreading skies.

VI.

In the isles of the Tyrrhenian sea
    Saint Patrick some period awaits,
And as canon with German he reads,
    As his history still to us states

VII.

To Hibernia Saint Patrick returned,
    By visions from angels induced;
For visions to him appeared oft,
    And his mind to subjection reduced.

VIII.

Soul-saving was Patrick's intent,
    For 'twas to far Foclut's dark flood;
He had heard the entreaty and wail
    Of children in Foclut's far woods.

IX.

For asked they the saint to make haste
    And Letavia's wide lands desert,
That from error's dark ways Eire's men
    He might in life's pathways direct.

X.

Foretold Eire's seers years of peace,
    Which were to remain through all time;
But the grandeurs of Tara the proud
    Were to vanish in dust, as earth's slime.

XI.

To Leary, the monarch, Druids told
    Of the advent of Patrick the saint;
And their visions were true, as we know
    From the facts which his histories paint.

XII.

Renowned was Saint Patrick through life,
    And of error he was a dire foe;
Hence for ever his name shall be grand
    Among the nations, as ages shall flow.

Metrical Life of St. Patrick

XIII.

The Apocalypse sang he, and hymns,
    And three fifty full psalms, day by day;
He instructed and praised and baptized,
    And all time he continued to pray.

XIV.

Nor could any cold e'er prevent
    That he stayed in the water o'er nights;
And to gain the grand kingdom of heaven,
    Through the day he used preach on the heights.

XV.

By the far-famed fount of the North,
    Benibarka! thy waters sha'n't cease;
For a hundred full psalms he used sing
    Each night the Lord's praise to increase.

XVI.

Then he slept on a cold bed of stone,
    And with a wet cover was dressed;
A stone was his pillow each night –
    Such, such was the saint's nightly rest.

XVII.

To the people the Gospel was preached,
    With power and with miracles signed;
The blind and the lepers were cured,
    And Death his dead subjects resigned.

XVIII.

Saint Patrick did preach to the Scots,
    And in Letavia much he endured,
That whom he had won to the Lord
    In Judgment's dread day be secured.

XIX.

Emir's and proud Erimon's sons
    A demon contrived to ensnare;
And them did dread Satan engulf
    In the dark, fearful depths of his lair,

XX.

Until our apostle arrived,
    Who rescued and set them all free,
Through sixty long years of his life
    To Christ's cross the brave Fenians flee.

XXI.

Great darkness o'er Eire was spread,
    And its people their idols adored,
Nor in the true Godhead believed,
    Nor the Trinity, too, of the Lord.

XXII.

At Armagh the realm's throne has been placed,
    To Emania a glory to be;
And far-famed is Dundalethglas church,
    Nor let fame from Temoria flee.

XXIII.

To Armagh, in his infirm old age,
    Saint Patrick desired much to go;
But God's angel at noon met the saint,
    And induced him his wish to forego.

XXIV.

Southward to the angel he came
    (For Victor had been his good guide),
And the bush in which Victor appeared
    Burned bright, and a voice from it cried:

XXV.

"At Armagh let the government be,
    And to Christ let all glory be brought;
Indeed, thou shalt come unto heaven;
    Thou obtainedst, because thou hadst sought.

XXVI.

"A hymn which you sing while alive
    Shall to Celts a proud armament be;
And at judgment the Irish surround
    Their father, their patron, in thee."

XXVII.

After Patrick, good Tassach remained;
    When Patrick to Tassach Christ gave,
Tassach said: "He from me shall receive";
    And the prediction of Tassach was grave.

XXVIII.

For the night was installed a bright day,
    And that day for one year did remain;
So that over all Eire the fair
    Light's brilliance and brightness did reign.

XXIX.

Bethoron a battle beheld
    Of great Nun against Chanaan's sons,
In which Gabaon saw the sun stand,
    As the Scriptural narrative runs.

XXX.

For brave Josue stood the bright sun
    To witness the wicked all slain;
Why not for Saint Patrick thrice more
    To illumine Hibernia's plain?

XXXI.

For all Eire's good clergy were come
    To bury Saint Patrick with pride;
And the sounds of the singing from heaven
    Cast them sleeping all round, far and wide.

XXXII.

Saint Patrick's pure soul fled his frame
    (His works immortality make);
And on the first night after death,
    The angels of God watched his wake.

XXXIII.

And when Patrick departed from life,
  To the other Saint Patrick came he;
And to Jesus, of Mary the Son,
  The two passed, bright and pure, great and free.

XXXIV.

In Patrick pride's stain was not found;
  And great were the works that adorn
This good son of Christ, Mary's Son!
  With God's blessing Saint Patrick was born.

TRIPARTITE LIFE OF ST. PATRICK

PART I.

The people who sat in darkness saw a great light, and they who were in the land and in the shadow of death received light by which came their illumination.

Patrick, then, was of the Britons of Alcluaid by origin. Calpurnn was his father's name. He was a noble priest. Potid was his grandfather's name, whose title was a deacon. Conceis was his mother's name. She was of the Franks, and a sister to Martin. In Nemtur, moreover, the man St. Patrick was born; and the flag (stone) on which St. Patrick was born would give forth water when any one swore a false oath upon it, as if it were lamenting the false testimony. If the oath was true, however, the stone would continue in its natural condition.

When the man St. Patrick was born, he was taken to a blind, flat-faced man to be baptized. Gornias was the priest's name; and he had no water out of which he could perform the baptism until he made the sign of the cross over the ground with the infant's hand, when a fountain of water burst forth. Gornias washed his face, and his eyes were opened to him; and he, who had learned no letter, read the baptism. God wrought three miracles through Patrick in this place—viz., the fountain of water through the ground, his eyesight to the blind man, and his reading the *ordo* of the baptism without knowing a letter up to that time. And Patrick was subsequently baptized. A church was founded, moreover, over this well in which Patrick was baptized; and the well is at the altar, and it has the form of the cross, as the learned report.

Many prodigies and miracles were wrought through Patrick in his youth, but we shall only relate a few out of many of them. One time Patrick was in his nurse's house, in winter time, when a great flood and rain filled his nurse's residence, so that the vessels and furniture of the house were floating about, and the fire was extinguished. Patrick then cried to his nurse, as usual with children when desiring food. Then his nurse said to him: "That is not what troubles us; there is something else we would rather do than to prepare food for thee; even the fire is extinguished." When Patrick heard these words, truly, he sought a certain spot in the house to which the water had not reached; and he dipped his hand in the water, and five drops fell from Patrick's fingers, and they were suddenly changed into five sparks, and the fire glowed, and the water rose not. The names of God and of Patrick were magnified thereby. Another time, as Patrick was playing amongst his companions, in the time of winter and cold in particular, he collected his armful of pieces of ice, which he brought home to his nurse. Then his nurse said: "It would be better for you to bring us withered brambles to warm ourselves with than what you have brought." Thereupon he said to his nurse:

"Believe thou, because God is powerful thereto, that even the sheets of ice will burn like faggots." And no sooner were the pieces of ice placed on the fire, and he had breathed on them, than they burned like faggots. The names of God and Patrick were magnified through this miracle.

One time, when Patrick and his sister (*i.e.*, Lupait) were herding sheep, the lambs came suddenly to their dams, as is customary with them, to drink milk. When Patrick and his sister saw this, they ran quickly to prevent them. The girl fell, and her head struck against a stone, so that death was nigh unto her. As soon as Patrick perceived that his sister was lying down, and that death was nigh unto her, he wept loudly; and he raised her up immediately, and made the sign of the cross over the wound, and it healed without any illness. (Nevertheless, the signs of the "white wound" would appear there.) And they came home as if no evil had happened to them. Another time, Patrick was with the sheep, when a wolf took away a sheep from him. His nurse reproved him greatly therefor. The wolf brought the sheep whole to the same place on the morrow; and the restoration in this way was wonderful—viz., the wolf's dislike regarding the habitual food.

Part I

When Patrick's nurse, therefore, saw him magnified by God in prodigies and miracles, she used to love him very much, and would not wish to go anywhere without him. One time his nurse went to milk the cow. He went with her to get a drink of new milk. The cow [became mad] in the *booley*, and killed five other cows. The nurse was much grieved, and asked him to resuscitate the cows. He resuscitated the cows, then, so that they were quite well, and he cured the mad cow; and the names of God and Patrick were magnified through this miracle.

There was a great assembly held by the Britons. He went to the assembly with his nurse and his guardian. It happened that his guardian died in the assembly. All were hushed into silence thereat; and his relatives cried, and his friends wept, and they said, "Why, thou *gilla*, didst thou let the man who was carrying thee die?" As regards the *gilla* moreover, he ran to his guardian, and placed his hands about his neck, and said to him, "Arise, and let us go home." He arose forthwith at Patrick's word, and they went home safe afterwards.

The boys of the place in which Patrick was nursed were wont to bring honey to their mothers from the bees' nests. Then his nurse said to Patrick: "Although every other boy brings honey to his nurse, you bring none to me." Patrick afterwards carried off a bucket to the water, and filled it, and blessed the water, so that it changed into honey; and it healed every disease and ailment to which it was applied.

One time the King of Britain's steward went to command Patrick and his nurse to go and clean the hearth of the royal house in Al-Cluaid. Patrick and his nurse went. Then it was that the angel came, and said to Patrick: "Pray, and it will not be necessary for you to perform that work." Patrick prayed. The angel afterwards cleaned the hearth. Then Patrick said: "Though all the firewood in Britain were burned in that fireplace, there would be no ashes of it on the morrow." And this, indeed, is fulfilled yet. Another time, the King of Britain's steward went to demand tribute of curds and butter from Patrick's nurse; and she had nothing that she would give for the rent. Then it was that Patrick made curds and butter of the snow, and they were taken to the king; and the moment they were exhibited to the king, afterwards they changed into the nature of snow again. The king thereupon forgave the rent to Patrick for ever.

The cause of Patrick's coming to Erinn was as follows: The seven sons of Fechtmad—viz., the seven sons of the King of Britain—were on a naval expedition, and they went to plunder in Armoric-Letha; and a number of the Britons of Srath-Cluaidh were on a visit

Tripartite Life of St. Patrick

with their kinsmen, the Britons of Armoric-Letha, and Calpurn, son of Potit, Patrick's father, and his mother—*i.e.*, Conches, daughter of Ocbas of the Galls—*i.e.*, of the Franks—were killed in the slaughter in Armorica. Patrick and his two sisters—viz., Lupait and Tigris—were taken prisoners, moreover, in that slaughter. The seven sons of Fechtmad went afterwards on the sea, having with them Patrick and his two sisters in captivity. The way they went was around Erinn, northwards, until they landed in the north; and they sold Patrick to Miliuc, son of Buan—*i.e.*, to the King of Dal-Araidhe. They sold his sisters in Conaille-Muirthemhne. And they did not know this. Four persons, truly, that purchased him. One of them was Miliuc. It was from this that he received the name that is Cothraige, for the reason that he served four families. He had, indeed, four names. . . .

[Here a leaf is missing from both the Bodleian and British Museum MSS. of the Tripartite Life, the contents of which would fill eight pages of similar size to the foregoing.]

When Patrick had completed his sixtieth year, and had learned knowledge, his auxiliary angel, Victor (for he was of assistance to him when he [Patrick] was in bondage with Miliuc, and regarding everything besides which he might wish), went to him, and said to him: "You are commanded from God to go to Erinn, to strengthen faith and belief, that you may bring the people, by the net of the Gospel, to the harbor of life; for all the men of Erinn call out your name, and they think it seasonable and fit that you should come." Patrick afterwards bade farewell to Germanus, and gave him a blessing; and a trusted senior went with him from Germanus, to guard him and testify for him; his name was Segetius, and he was by grade a priest, and he it was who usually kept the *Ordo* of the church besides Germanus.

Patrick went subsequently on the sea, his company being nine. Then he went upon an island, where he saw a withered old woman on her hands at the door of a house. "Whence is the hag?" asked Patrick; "great is her infirmity." A young man answered, and said: "She is a descendant of mine," said the young man; "if you could see the mother of this girl, O cleric! she is more infirm still." "In what way did this happen?" enquired Patrick. "Not difficult to tell," said the young man. "We are here since the time of Christ. He came to visit us when He was on earth amongst men; and we made a feast for him, and he blessed our house and blessed ourselves; but this blessing reached not our children; and we shall be here without age or decay for ever. And it is long since thy coming was foretold to us," said the young man; "and God 'left it with us' [*i.e.*, prophesied to us] that thou wouldst come to preach to the Gaeidhel; and He left a token with us, *i.e.*, His *bachall* (crozier), to be given to thee." "I will not take it," said Patrick, "until He Himself gives me His *bachall*." Patrick remained three days and three nights with them; and he went afterwards into Sliabh-Hermoin, near the island, where the Lord appeared unto him, and commanded him to go and preach to the Gaeidliel; and He gave him the Bachall-Isa, and said that it would be of assistance to him in every danger and every difficulty in which he would be. And Patrick besought three requests of him—viz., (1) to be at His right hand in the kingdom of heaven; (2) that he (Patrick) might be the judge of the Gaeidhel on the Day of Judgment; and (3) as much as the nine companions could carry of gold and silver to give to the Gaeidhel for believing.

The Airchinnech that was in Rome at that time was Celestinus, the forty-second man from Peter. He sent Palladius, a high deacon, with twelve men, to instruct the Gaeidhel (for to the comarb of Peter belongs the instruction of Europe), in the same way as Barnabas went from Peter to instruct the Romans, etc. When Palladius arrived in the territory of Leinster—*i.e.*, at Inbher-Dea—Nathi, son of Garchu, opposed him, and expelled him. And Palladius baptized a few there, and founded three churches—viz., Cill-fine (in which he left his books, and the casket with the relics of Paul and Peter, and the tablet in which he used to write), and Tech-na-Roman, and Doinhnach-Airte, in which Silvester and Solonius are. On turning back afterwards, sickness seized him in the country of the Cruithne, and he died of it.

When Patrick heard this thing, and knew that it was for him God designed the apostleship of Erinn, he went subsequently to Rome to receive grade; and it was Celestinus, Abbot of Rome, who read *grada* (orders, degrees) over him; Germanus and Amatho, King of the Romans, being present with them.

When Patrick came from Rome, where he arrived was at Inbher-Dea, in Leinster. Nathi, son of Garchu, came also against him. Patrick cursed him. Sinell, moreover, the son of Finnchadh, was the first who believed in Erinn through Patrick's teaching. Hence it was that Patrick blessed him and his seed. On the same day Auxilius and Eserninus, and others of Patrick's people, were ordained; and it was then, also, that the name Patricius—*i.e.*, a name of power with the

Tripartite Life of St. Patrick

Romans—was given to him; *i.e.*, a hostage-liberating man. It was he, moreover, who loosened the hostageship and bondage of the Gaeidhel to the devil. And when they were reading the *grada* (orders, degrees), the three choirs responded—viz., the choir of the men of heaven, and the choir of the Romans, and the choir of the children from the woods of Fochlud—all whom cried out, "Hibernienses omnes," etc. In illis diebus autem gesta sunt in predictis ita. In that time there was a fierce pagan king in Erinn—*i.e.*, Laeghaire Mac Neill—and his seat and royal hold was in Tara. In the fifth year of the reign of Laeghaire Mac Neill Patrick came to Erinn. The eighth year of the reign of Lughaidh he died. The eighth year of the reign of Theodosius, the forty-fifth man from Augustus, Patrick came; eight years Celestine was then prince, as Gelasius said.

This valiant king, then—*i.e.*, Laeghaire Mac Neill—possessed druids and enchanters, who used to foretell through their druidism and through their paganism what was in the future for them. Lochru and Luchat Mael were their chiefs; and these two were authors of that art of pseudo-prophecy. They prophesied, then, that a mighty, unprecedented prophet would come across the sea, with an unknown code of instructions, with a few companions, whom multitudes would obey, and who would obtain dignity and reverence from the men of Erinn; and that he would expel kings and princes from their governments, and would destroy all the idolatrous images; and that the faith which would arrive would live for ever in Erin. Two years, or three, before the arrival of Patrick, what they used to prophesy was [as follows];

> "A *Tailcend* (*i.e.*, Patrick) shall come across the stormy sea.
> His garment head-pierced, his staff head-bent,
> His *mias* (*i.e.*, altar) in the east of his house;
> His people all shall answer, Amen, amen."

Baile-Cuinn (the Ecstasy of Conn, a rhapsody so called) dixit: "A *Tailcend* shall come who will found cemeteries, make cells new, and pointed music-houses, with conical caps [bencopar], and have princes bearing croziers." "When these signs shall come," said they, "our adoration and our *gentility* (paganism) will vanish, and faith and belief will be magnified." As it was foretold then and represented, so it happened and was fulfilled.

When Patrick completed his voyage, and his ship entered the harbor at Inbher-Dea, in the territory of Leinster, he brought his ships to the shore. Then it was that he decided to go to instruct Miliuc. He thought fit as he labored at first for his body, that he should labor for his soul. He then put stick to shore, and proceeded on a prosperous voyage, past the coast of Erinn, eastwards, until he stopped in Inbher-Domnand. He found no fish there, and cursed it. He went to Inis-Patrick: and he sent to Inbher-Nainge, where nothing was found for him. He cursed this also, and both are unfruitful. Then it was that Benen came into his company. Soon after, Patrick slept awhile, and all the odoriferous flowers that the youth could find, he would put them into the cleric's bosom. Patrick's people said to Benen: "Stop doing that, lest thou shouldst awake Patrick." Patrick said: "He will be the heir of my kingdom." He went to Inbher-Boindi, where he found fish. He blessed it, and the *Inbher* is fruitful. He found druids in that place who denied the virginity of Mary. Patrick blessed the ground, and it swallowed the druids. Patrick went afterwards from Inis-Patrick, past Conaille, and past the coast of Ulster, until he stopped at Inbher-Brena. He went afterwards to Inbher-Slani, where the clerics hid their ships; and they went ashore to put off their fatigue, and to rest; so that there it was the swine-herd of Dichu, son of Trichim, found them, where Sabhall-Patrick is to-day. When he saw the divines and the clerics, he thought they were robbers or thieves, and he went to tell his lord; whereupon Dichu came, and set his dog at the clerics. Then it was that Patrick uttered the prophetic verse, "*Ne tradas bestis, etc., et canis obmutuit.*" When Dichu saw Patrick, he became gentle, and he believed, and Patrick baptized him; so that he was the first in Ulster who received faith and baptism from Patrick. Then it was that Dichu presented the Sabhall to Patrick. Patrick said:

> "The blessing of God on Dichu,
> Who gave to me the Sabhall;
> May he be hereafter
> Heavenly, joyous, glorious.
> "The blessing of God on *Dichu*--
> Dichu with full folds (flocks);
> No one of his sept or kindred
> Shall die, except after a long life."

Patrick went to preach to Miliuc, as we have said, and took gold with him to prevail on him to believe; for he knew that he (Miliuc) was covetous regarding gold. But when Miliuc heard that Patrick had arrived, he wished not to believe for him, and to abandon the pagan religion. He thought it unbecoming to believe for his servant, and

Tripartite Life of St. Patrick

to submit to him. The counsel that a demon taught him was this: He went into his royal house with his gold and silver; and he set the house on fire, and was burned with all his treasures, and his soul went to hell. Then it was that Patrick proceeded past the northern side of Sliabh-Mis (there is a cross in that place), and he saw the fire afar off. He remained silent for the space of two or three hours, thinking what it could be, and he said, "That is the fire of Miliuc's house," said Patrick, "after his burning himself in the middle of his house, that he might not believe in God in the end of his life. As regards the man who persuaded him thereto," added he, "there shall not be a king or righdamhna of his family, and his seed and race shall be 'in service' for ever, and his soul shall not return from hell to the judgment, nor after judgment." After he had said these words, he turned *deisel* (right-hand-wise) and went back again into the territory of Uladh, until he arrived at Magh-inis, to Dichu, son of Trichim, and he remained there a long time disseminating faith, so that he brought all the Ulidians, with the net of the Gospel, to the harbor of life.

Patrick went subsequently from Sabhall southwards, that he might preach to Ros, son of Trichim. He it was that resided in Derlus, to the south of Dun-leth-glaise (Downpatrick). There is a small city (cathair, *i.e.*, *civitas*, but also meaning a bishop's *see*) there this day— *i.e.*, Brettain, *ubi est Episcopus Loarn qui ausus est increpare Patricium tenentem manum pueri ludentis justa Ecclesiam suam*. As Patrick was then on his way, he saw a tender youth herding pigs. Mochae his name. Patrick preached to him, and baptized him, and cut his hair, and gave him a copy of the gospels and a reliquary. And he gave him also, another time, a *bachall* which had been given them from God—viz., its head into Patrick's bosom, and its end in Mochae's bosom; and this is the Detech-Mochae of Noendruim; and Mochae promised Patrick a shorn pig every year. And this, indeed, is still given.

When the solemnity of Easter approached, Patrick considered that there was no place more suitable to celebrate the high solemnity of the year—*i.e.*, the Easter—than in Magh-Bregh, the place where the head of the idolatry and druidism of Erinn was—viz., in Temhair. They afterwards bade farewell to Dichu, son of Trichim, and put their vessels on the sea; and they proceeded until they anchored in Inbher-Colptha. They left their vessels in the Inbher, and went by land until they reached Ferta-fer-féc, and Patrick's tent was fixed in this place, and he cut the Easter fire. It happened, however, that this was the time in which the great festival of the Gentiles—*i.e.*, the *Fes of Tara*—was usually celebrated. The kings and princes and chieftains were wont to come to Laeghaire Mac Neill to Tara, to celebrate this festival. The druids and the magicians were also wont to come to prophesy to them. The fire of every hearth in Erinn was usually extinguished on that night, and it was commanded by the king that no fire should be lighted in Erinn before the fire of Tara, and neither gold nor silver would be accepted from any one who would light it, but he should suffer death for it. Patrick knew not this thing; and if he knew it, it would not prevent him.

As the people of Tara were thus, they saw the consecrated Easter fire at a distance which Patrick had lighted. It illuminated all Magh-Bregh. Then the king said: "That is a violation of my prohibition and law; and do you ascertain who did it." "We see the fire," said the druids, "and we know the night in which it is made. If it is not extinguished before morning," added they, "it will never be extinguished. The man who lighted it will surpass the kings and princes, unless he is prevented." When the king heard this thing, he was much infuriated. Then the king said: "That is not how it shall be; but we will go," said he, "until we slay the man who lighted the fire." His chariot and horses were yoked for the king, and they went, in the end of the night, to Ferta-fer-féc. "You must take care," said the druids, "that you go not to the place where the fire was made, lest you worship the man who lighted it; but stay outside, and let him be called out to you, that he may know you to be a king, and himself a subject; and we will argue in your presence." "It is good counsel," said the king; "it shall be done as you say." They proceeded afterwards until they unyoked their horses and chariots in front of the *Ferta*. Patrick was "whispered" out to them; and it was commanded by them that no one should rise up before him, lest he should believe in him. Patrick rose and went out; and when he saw the chariots and horses unyoked, he sang the prophetic stanza:

> "Hi in curribus et hi in eorus (equis),
> Nos autem, in nomine Domini Dei nostri ma."

They were then before him, and the rims of their shields against their chins; and none of them rose up before him, except one man alone, in whom was a figure from God—*i.e.*, Ere, son of Dega. He is the Bishop Ere who is [commemorated] in Slaine of Magh-Bregh to-day. Patrick blessed him, and he believed in God, and confessed the Catholic faith, and was baptized; and Patrick said to him: "Your seat (*cathair*, chair or city) on earth shall be noble"; and Pat-

Tripartite Life of St. Patrick

rick's (*comarb*) successor is bound to bend the knee before his *comarb* in consideration of his submission.

Each then questioned the other—viz., Patrick and Laeghaire. Lochru went fiercely, enviously, with contention and questions, against Patrick; and then he began to denounce the Trinity and the Catholic faith. Patrick looked severely at him, and cried out to God with a loud voice, and he said: *"Domine qui omnia potes et in tua potestate consistit quidquid est, quique nos misisti huc ad nomen tuum gentibus praedicandum hic impius qui blasphemat nomen tuum, elevatur nunc foras, et cito moriatur. Et his dictis elevatus est magus in aëra et iterum desuper cito dejectus sparso ad lapidem cerebro comminutus et mortus fuerat coram eis."* The pagans became afraid at this. But the king was much infuriated against Patrick, and he determined to kill him. He told his people to slay the cleric. When Patrick observed this thing—the rising up against him of the pagans—he cried out with a loud voice, and said: *"Et exurget Deus et dissipentur inimici ejus, et fugiant qui oderunt eum a facie ejus, sicut defecit fumus deficit sic deficiant sicut fluit caera a facie ignis; sic pereint peccatorus facie Domini."* Immediately darkness went over the sun, and great shaking and trembling of the earth occurred. They thought it was heaven that fell upon the earth; and the horses started off, frightened, and the wind blew the chariots across the plains, and all rose against each other in the assembly; and they were all attacking each other, so that fifty men of them fell in this commotion through Patrick's malediction. The Gentiles fled in all directions, so that only three remained—viz., Laeghaire, and his queen, and a man of his people; *et timuerunt valde, veniensque regina ad Patricium* (*i.e.*, Angass, daughter of Tassagh, son of Liathan), *dixit*: *"Ei homo juste et potens ne perdas regem.* The king will go to thee, and will submit to thee, and will kneel, and will believe in God." Laeghaire went then, and knelt before Patrick, and gave him a "false peace." Not long after this, the king beckoned Patrick aside, and what he meditated was to kill him; but this happened not, because God had manifested this intention to Patrick. Laeghaire said to Patrick, "Come after me, O cleric! to Tara, that I may believe in thee before the men of Erinn"; and he then placed men in ambush before Patrick in every pass from Ferta-fer-féc to Tara, that they might kill him. But God did not permit it. Patrick went, accompanied by eight young clerics (*maccleirech*), and Benen as a *gilla*, along with them; and Patrick blessed them before going, and a *dicheltair* (garment of invisibility) went over them, so that not one of them was seen. The Gentiles who were in the ambuscades, however, saw eight wild deer going past them along the mountain, and a young fawn after them, and a pouch on his shoulder—viz., Patrick, and his eight [clerics], and Benen after them, and his (Patrick's) *polaire* (satchel, or epistolary) on his back.

Laeghaire went afterwards, about twilight, to Tara, in sorrow and shame, with the few persons who escaped in his company. On the day succeeding Easter Sunday the men of Erinn went to Tara to drink the feast; for the *Fes* of Tara was a principal day with them. When they were banqueting, and thinking of the conflict they waged the day before, they saw Patrick, who arrived in the middle of Tara, *januis clausis ut Christus in cennaculum*; because Patrick meditated: "I will go," said he, "so that my readiness may be manifested before the men of Erinn. I shall not make a candle under a bushel of myself. I will see," said he, "who will believe me, and who will not believe me." No one rose up before him inside but *Dubhtach* Mac Ua Lugair alone, the king's royal poet, and a tender youth of his people (viz., his name was Fiacc; it is he who is [commemorated] in Slebhte to-day). This Dubhtach, truly, was the first man who believed that day in Tara. Patrick blessed him and his seed. Patrick was then called to the king's bed, that he might eat food, and to prove him in prophecy (*i.e.*, in Venturis rebus). Patrick did not refuse this, because he knew what would come of it. The druid Luchat Mael went to drink with him, for he wished to revenge on Patrick what he had done to his (the druid's) companion the day before. The druid Luchat Mael put a drop of poison into the goblet which was beside Patrick, that he might see what Patrick would do in regard to it. Patrick observed this act, and he blessed the goblet, and the ale adhered to it, and he turned the goblet upside-down afterwards, and the poison which the druid put into it fell out of it. Patrick blessed the goblet again, and the ale changed into its natural state. The names of God and Patrick were magnified thereby. The hosts then went and took up their station outside Tara. "Let us work miracles," said Luchat Mael, "before the multitude in this great plain." Patrick asked; "What are they?" The druid said: "Let us bring snow upon the plain, so that the plain may be white before us." Patrick said to him: "I do not wish to go against the will of God." The druid said: "I will bring the snow upon the plain, though you like it not." He then began the druidic poetry and the demoniacal arts until the snow fell so that it would reach the girdles of men; and all saw and wondered greatly. Patrick said: "We see this; send it away, if you can." The druid answered: "I cannot do that thing until this time to-morrow." "By my *debhro*," said Patrick, "in evil is thy power, and not in good." Patrick blessed the plain before him, towards the four points, and the snow immediately disappeared, without rain, without sun, without wind, at Patrick's word. Darkness afterwards went over the face of the earth, through the incantations of the druid. The multitudes cried out thereat. Patrick said: *"Expelli tenebras."* The druid answered: "I am not able to-day." Patrick prayed the Lord, and blessed the plain, and the darkness was expelled, and the sun shone out, and all gave thanks. They were for a long time contending thus before the king—*i.e.*, as Nero said to Simon and Peter—*et ait rex ad illos, "Libros vestros in aqua mittite, et ilium cujus libri illesi evaserint adorabimus." Respondit Patricius: "Faciam ego"; et dixit magus: "Nolo ego ad judicium ire aquae cum ipso; aquam etiam Deum habet";* because he heard that it was through water Patrick used to baptize. *Et respondit rex: "Mittite igitur in igne"; et ait Patricius: "Promptus sum;"* at *magus nolens dixit; "Hic homo versa vice in alternos annos nunc aquam nunc ignem deum veneratur."* "It is not this that shall be done," said Patrick; "for since you say that it is the fire I adore, go you, if you wish, into a house apart, and well closed, and a student of my people along with you, and let my *casula* be about you, and your druidic tunic about my student (*mac cleirech*); and fire will be applied to the house, that God may decide between you there." This counsel was agreed to by the men of Erinn, including Laeghaire. The house was then made, one-half of dry faggots, and the other half of fresh materials. The druid was put into the fresh part, and Patrick's *casula* about him. Benen, however, was put into the dry part, with the druid's tunic about him. The house was afterwards closed and fastened on the outside, before the multitude, and fire was applied to it. A great prodigy occurred there through Patrick's prayers. The fresh part of the house was burned, as well as the druid under the casula, and not a bit of the *casula* was destroyed. The dry portion, in which was Benen, however, was not burned, and God preserved Benen under the druid's tunic, and the tunic was burned, so that it was reduced to ashes. The king was greatly enraged against Patrick for the killing of his druid. He arose, and would like to slay Patrick; but God did not permit it, through the intercession of Patrick. The anger of God fell afterwards on the impious multitude, so that great numbers of them died—viz., twelve thousand in one day. Patrick said to Laeghaire: "If you do not believe now, you shall die quickly; for the anger of God will come upon your head." When the king heard these words, he was seized with great fear. The king went into a house afterwards to take counsel with his people. "It is better for me," said he, "to believe in God than [to suffer] what is threatened to

Part I

me—my death." It was after this that Laeghaire knelt to Patrick, and believed in God, and many thousands believed in that day.

Then it was that Patrick said to Laeghaire: "Since you have believed in God, and have submitted to me, length of life in thy sovereignty will be given thee. As a reward for thy disobedience some time ago, however, there will be no king nor roydamhna from thee for ever, except Lughaidh," the son of Laeghaire; for his mother implored Patrick that he would not curse the infant that was in her womb, when Patrick said: "I will not, until he comes against me." Lughaidh then assumed the sovereignty; and he went to Achadh-farcha. There he said: "Is not that the church of the cleric who said that there would be neither king nor roydamhna from Laeghaire?" After this, darts of lightning descended from the heavens on his head, which killed him, and hence is [the name] Achadh-farcha. These miracles live to this day. These are the miracles the divines of Erinn knew, and through which they put a thread of narration. Columcille, son of Fedhlidhmidh, Ultan, the grand-son of Conchobhar, Adamnan, the grandson of Tinne, Eleran the Wise, Ciaran of Belach-duin, Cruimther Collait from Druim-Railgech, knew Patrick's miracles in the first place, and composed them.

A man of truth, indeed, was this man, with purity of mind like the Patriarchs; a true pilgrim like Abraham; gentle and forgiving of heart like Moses; a praise-singing psalmist like David; a shrine of wisdom like Solomon; a chosen vessel for proclaiming truth like Paul the Apostle; a man full of grace and knowledge of the Holy Ghost like John; the root of a holy herb-garden towards the children of faith; a vine branch with fruitfulness; a sparkling fire, with power to heat and warm the sons of life, in founding and dispensing charity. A lion in strength and might; a dove in gentleness and humility. A serpent in wisdom and cunning in regard to good; gentle, humble, mild, towards sons of life; dark, ungentle, towards sons of death. A slave in work and labor for Christ; a king in dignity and power, for binding and releasing, for enslaving and freeing, for killing and reviving.

Appropinquante autem hora obitus sui, sacrificium ab Episcopo Tassach sumpsit quod viaticum vitae aeternae ex consilio Victoris acceperat, et deinceps post mortuos suscitatos, post multum populum ad Deum conversum, et post Episcopos et presbyteros in ecclesiis ordinatos, et toto ordine Ecclesiastico conversa tota Scotia ad fidem Christi, anno aetatis suae cxii. obdormivit in vitam aeternam.

PART II.

Euntes ergo docete omnes gentes baptizantes eos in nomine Patris, et Filii, et Spiritus Sancti, docentes eos observare omnia quaecumque mandavi vobis, etc.

When Patrick came with his fleet to Erinn, to preach to the Gaeidhel, and went to Tara, he left Lomman in Inbher-Boinne, to take care of his ships, during the forty nights of the Lent. Patrick commanded him to row his vessel against the [current of the] Boyne, until he would arrive at the place were to-day Ath-Truim [Trim] is—at that time the *dún* of Fedhlimidh, where he (Lomman) found the son of Laeghaire MacNeill—*i.e.*, at Ath-Truim. And in the morning, Fortchern, Fedhlimidh's son, went and found Lomman, and his gospels before him. He wondered at the precepts he heard. He believed, and was baptized by Lomman. And Fortchern was listening to the instruction, until his mother went to seek him. She welcomed the clerics, for she was of the Britons, viz.: Scoth, daughter of the king of Britain. Fedhlimidh himself came to converse with Lomman; and he believed, and presented Ath-Truim to God and Patrick, and to Lomman, and to Fortchern. Patrick himself went and founded Ath-Truim [Trim], twenty-five years before the foundation of Ard-Macha. Of the Britons, moreover, was the origin of Lomman, and his mother was the sister of Patrick.

Lomman's brethren were, moreover, Bishop Munis in Forgnidhe in Cuircne—*i.e.*, in the north of Meath, to the south of the Ethne (Inny); Broccaidh in Imlech-Achaidh, in Ciarraighe of Connacht; Broccan in Brechmagh, in Ui-Dorthain; Mughenoc in Cill-Dumagloin, in the south of Bregia. They were the relatives, moreover, who were dear to Patrick by consanguinity, and faith, and baptism, and instruction; and they presented to Patrick whatever they possessed, land and churches, for ever. But, after some time, when Lomman's death drew nigh, Lomman and his foster-son, *i.e.*, Fortchern, went to converse with his brother, *i.e.*, Broccaid, and he committed his church to Patrick and Fortchern; and Fortchern opposed it, that he might not inherit his father's possessions, who gave the place to God and Patrick. But Lomman said, "You shall not receive my benediction unless you assume the abbacy of my church." Fortchern took upon him the abbacy after the death of Lomman, for three days, when he went to Trim; and afterwards gave his church to Cathlai, a pilgrim. These are the offerings of Fedhlimidh, son of Laeghaire, to St. Patrick, and to Lomman, and to Fortchern, viz., Ath-Truim, in the territory of Laeghaire of Bregia, and Imghae, in the territory of Laeghaire of Meath. The way in which all these offerings were presented to Patrick, and to Lomman, and to Fortchernd, *per* (sic) *omnibus regibus majoribus et minoribus usque indiem judicii. Prima feria venit Patricius ad Taltenam*, where the regal assembly was, to Cairpre, the son of Niall. It was he who desired the murder of Patrick, and who drove Patrick's people into the river Sele, wherefore Patrick called him the enemy of God, and said to him, "Thy seed shall serve thy brother's seed," and there shall not be salmon in that river, through Patrick's malediction. Patrick went afterwards to Conall, the son of Niall, whose residence was where Donagh-Patrick is this day, who received him with great joy; and Patrick baptized him, and confirmed his royal seat for ever. And Patrick said to him: "Thy brother's seed shall serve thy seed for ever; and strive to exercise charity towards my successors after me, and the sons of thy sons, that they may be perpetual subjects to my sons of faith." Then it was that Conall measured a church for God and Patrick, sixty feet in extent; and Patrick said: "Whichsoever of your race diminishes this church shall not have a long reign, and he shall not be prosperous." They went early on Sunday morning to Rath-Airthir, Cinaed and Dubhdaleithe, the two sons of Cerbhall, son of Maelodhra, son of Aedh-Slaine, when they saw a young man lying down—*i.e.*, the son of Bresal. One of them plunged a sword into him, and then throttled him. The murderer then went past Tailten, up, on his straight road, and the other went to Domnach-Patrick. It was then that Patrick blessed that part of the plain of Tailte, so that dead bodies are never borne off from it.

[A few lines of the MS. at this place are damaged.]

The Pasch being therefore finished, on the next day Patrick came to *vadum duarum forcarum* (Ath-da-laarg, near Kells; county

Part II

Meath), and founded a church there, and left the three brothers there with their sister, viz., Cathaceus, and Cathurus, and Catnean; and Catnea, the sister, who used to milk the deer. He went afterwards to Druim Corcortri, and founded a church there, and he left in it Diarmaid, son of Restitutus.

When Patrick was going eastwards to Tara, to Laeghaire (for they had formed a friendship), from Domhnach-Patrick, he blessed Conall, son of Niall. When he was going away, he threw his flagstone (*lec*) behind him eastwards into the hill, *i.e.*, where ......

[A folio of the original MS. is missing here.]

And Maine knelt to Patrick and performed penance, and Patrick said, "*Rex non erit qui te non habebit*; and thy injunctions shall be the longest that will live in Erinn. The person whom I have blessed also shall be a king, *i.e.*, Tuathal [Maelgarbh]." And he [Tuathal] assumed the sovereignty afterwards, and banished Diarmaid MacCerbhaill, so that he was on *Loch-Ri*, and on *Derg-Derc*, and on *Luimnech*.

One day as Diarmaid went in his boat past the shore of Cluainmic-Nois, Ciaran heard the noise and motion of the craft, and called him ashore, and Ciaran said, "Come to me, for thou art a king's son, and mark out the Redes [a church] and the Eclais-bec [a little church], and grant the place to me." He said, "I am not a king." To whom Ciaran said, "You will be a king to-morrow." In that day, the king, Tuathal, came with great bands to banish Diarmaid, when Maelmor (of the Conaille), Diarmaid's foster-brother, killed him; and Maelmor was immediately slain. Hence the old saying, "the feat of Maelmor." Diarmaid afterwards assumed the sovereignty of Erinn, through Ciaran's blessing when Diarmaid was marking the site of Eclais-bec, and bowed down thrice. He went to Tara, and gave Ciaran an offering for every *tairlim*, along with Druimraithe. *Ocurrit nobis hic virtus etsi per ancificatione* [recte *anticipationem*].

Another time Patrick heard, through the malice of the vulgar, that Bishop Mel had sinned with his sister, for they were wont to be in the same house, praying to the Lord. When Bishop Mel saw Patrick coming towards him to Ard-Achadh [Ardagh] to reprove him, Bishop Mel went out to a hill to fish in the pools and furrows. When it was told to Patrick that he had caught a salmon in this way, Patrick uttered

Tripartite Life of St. Patrick

the famous saying: *"Seorsim viri et seorsim foeminae ne occasionem dare intirmis inveniantur et ne nomen Domini per nos blasphemetur, quid absit a nobis,"* for God does not assist any unjust, false man; *i.e., non temptabis Dominum Deum tuum.* Bishop Mel's sister then went with fire in her *casula,* Patrick then knew there was no sin between them, *dicens, "Seorsum feminis ne occasione dare infirmis inveniamur et ne non Domini per nos blasfemaretur quod absit a nobis, et sic reliquit eos,"* i.e., Bri-Leith between them: she in Druim-Cheu to the west of Bri-Leith; he (Bishop Mel) to the east of it, in Ard-Achadh.

Patrick went afterwards into northern Tethbha, *i.e.,* to the territory of Cairbre, where Granard was presented to him by the sons of Cairbre, and he left there Bishop Guessacht, son of Milchu, his fosterbrother, and the two sisters Emir, who first put up at Cluain-Bronaigh; and this is the reason why the sides of the churches are joined to each other; and it is the *airchinnech* (superior) of Granard that always ordains the head nun in Cluain-Bronaigh. The moment that Patrick blessed the veil on the aforesaid virgins, their four feet sank into the rock, and the traces exist in it always. Patrick went afterwards across the water to Magh-Slechta, where the arch-idol of Erinn was, *i.e.,* Cenn Cruach, made of gold and silver, surrounded by twelve other idols formed of bronze. When Patrick saw the idols from the waters called Guthard (*i.e.,* he raised his voice—*guth,* voice; *ard,* high), and when he approached it, he lifted his hand to lay the Bachall-Isa on it; but he could not, as the idol inclined over to its right side (for towards the south its face was turned), and the mark of the *bachall* lives yet in its left side, although the *bachall* did not leave Patrick's hand. And the ground swallowed the other twelve idols as far as their heads; and they are in that condition in commemoration of the prodigy. And he cursed the demon (idol), and banished him to hell; and he called all the people, with king Laeghaire, who worshipped the idols; and all saw him (the demon), and feared death unless Patrick would banish him to hell. His *graif* (fibula) fell from Patrick's garment whilst maintaining the conflict and valor against the idol. He cut away all the heath in the place until he found his *graif,* and no heath grows in that place, nor in the plain besides. And he founded a church in that place, *i.e.,* Domhnach-Maighe-Slecht, and left there Mabran Barbarus, Patrick's relative and prophet, and Patrick's well is there, *ubi baptizavit multos.* Patrick went afterwards into the territory of Connacht, over Snamhdaen, across the Shannon, where he found a ford, viz.: the land (bed of the river) rose up under Patrick in the ford, and the learned will yet find that *esker.* And Patrick landed (*i.e.,* on the Connacht side of the

Part II

Shannon) immediately, and then it was that Buadmael, Patrick's charioteer, died, and was buried there. Cill-Buaidhmael is the name (of the church), and it is appropriate to Patrick. When Laeghaire Mac Neill's druids (*i.e.*, Mael and Caplait, two brothers, who had fostered Laeghaire's two daughters, Ethne the Fair, and Feidelm the Red) heard all that Patrick had done, they brought thick darkness over all Magh-Nai, through the power of the demon, for the space of three days and three nights. Patrick thereupon prayed to God, and bent his knees, and blessed the plain, so that there was darkness for the druids, and light for all others. And he gave thanks to God, and all the darkness was banished from Magh-Ai. And they went past the Shannon to Duma-graidh, where he ordained Ailbhe, a noble priest, who is [commemorated] in Senchua in Ui-Ailella; and Patrick instructed him regarding a stone altar [which was] in the mountain of Ui-Ailella, underground, and four glass Chalices at its four corners: *et dixit cavendum ne frangerantur orae fossurae. Inter nepotes etiam Ailello fuit, et baptizavit Maineum sanctum quem ordinavit Episcopus Bronus filius Iccni qui est i Caisel-Irra, servus Dei socius Patricii.* Patrick went to Magh-glas, where he founded Cill-mor of Magh-glas; and he left two of his people there, viz., Conleng and Ercleng. *Deinde venit in fines Corcu-Achland*, to the south of Ui-Ailella, and to the north of Badhghna. There were two brothers there, viz., Id and Hono, who were druids. Hono asked Patrick, "What will you give me for this land?" Patrick answered "Eternity." Hono said, "You possess gold: give it to me for it." Patrick replied, "I have given much, but God will give more." He afterwards found a mass of gold in the place where the pigs had been rooting, and Patrick gave the mass of gold to him (*i.e.*, to Hono) for his land. Tir-in-brotha is its name now. *Dixit Patricius, "Nec rex eris nec de semine tuo regnabit in aeternum." Illius vero lacrimis misertus est Patricius, dicens, "Non erit rex quem tua progenies non jurabit," etc., quod impletur.* Cenel Maic Erce is the strongest and most powerful [sept] in Connacht, but they do not govern like high-kings. Ona, son of Aengus, son of Ere Derg (Ere the Red), son of Brian, *de quo* Ui-Honach, presented his house to Patrick; and Imlech-Onon was its name at that time: Ailfinn, moreover, [is its name] this day; from the *ail* (rock) taken out of the well which was made by Patrick in the fair green, and which is on the brink of the well, the place has been named. Et dixit illi Patricius: "Thy seed shall be blessed, and the palm of laics and clerics shall be of thee for ever, and the inheritance of this place shall belong to them." *Et posuit ibi Assicum et Bite filium fratris Assicus (Assici?) et Cipiam matrem Bitei. Episcopus Assicus sanctus episcopus, faber aereus Patricii:* and he made altars, and four-cornered book-cases, and four-cornered dishes, in honor of Patrick; and a four-cornered dish of them was in Ard-Macha, and another in Ailfinn, and another in Domnach-mor of Magli-Seola, on the altar of the holy bishop Felanus in Ui-Briuin-Seola, far westwards from Ailfinn. Assicus, however, fled northwards to Sliabh-Liag, in Tir-Boghaine, where he was on an island for seven years. And his monks sought him, and found him, after much trouble, in the mountain glens; and they brought him away with them; and Assicus died with them in the desert, and they buried him in Rath-Cunga, in Seirthe. And the king of that county gave to him, and to his monks after his death, the pasture of one hundred cows with their calves, and twenty oxen, as a perpetual offering; for he said that he would not again go to Magh-Ai, on account of the falsehood which had been said there of him. His remains are in Rath-Cunga, and to Patrick belongs the church, upon which the people of Colum-Cilleand of Ard-Sratha have encroached. Patrick went from Elphin to Dumacha (the mounds) of Ui-Ailella, and built a church there, *i.e.*, Senchell-Dumaighe, and he left Machet in it, and Cetchen, and Rodan, a noble priest, and Mathona, Benen's sister, who received the veil from Patrick and from Rodan, and who was a servitor to them.

When Patrick was at Dumha-graidh, ordaining the great multitude, he smiled. "What is that?" asked Benen. "Bron, and the monk Olcan," said Patrick, "who came towards me along Traig-Eothaili, and my foster-son, Mac-Erca, with them; a wave of the sea made a great dash, and tried to carry off the youth." This was a prophecy. He (Patrick) went through the territory of Ui-Oilella, and founded the church eastwards in Tamhnagh, and it was built by God and men: *et ipsa fecit amicitiam ad reliquias Assici Rodani; et successores eorum epulabantur invicem. Post hoc autem possuerunt episcopum Cairellum juxta sanctam Ecclesiam in Tamhnagh, quem ordinaverunt Episcopum Patricii, viz., Bronus et Biteus.* Patrick went afterwards to the fountain, *i.e.*, Clibech, on the slopes of Cruachan, at sunrise. The clerics sat down at the fountain. Laeghaire Mac Neill's two daughters, viz., Eithne the Fair, and Feidelm the Red, went early to the fountain to wash their hands, as they were wont to do, when they found the synod of clerics at the well, with white garments, and their books, before them. They wondered at the appearance of the clerics, and imagined they were *fir-sidhe*, or phantoms. They questioned Patrick. "Whence are you, and whither have you come? Is it from the *sidhe*? Are you gods?" Patrick said to them, "It would be better for you to believe in

Part II

God than to ask regarding our race." The elder daughter said, "Who is your God, and in what place is he, in heaven or in earth? is it under the earth, or on the earth, or in seas, or in streams, or in hills, or in valleys? Has He sons and daughters? has He gold and silver? Is there a profusion of every good in his kingdom? Tell us plainly how we shall see Him, and how is He to be loved, and how is He to be found. Is He young or old? or is He ever-living? Is He beautiful, or have many fostered His son, or is His daughter handsome, and dear to men of the world?" St. Patrick, full of the Holy Spirit, responded, "Our God is the God of all, the God of heaven and earth, the God of the seas and rivers, the God of the sun and moon, and all the other planets; the God of the high hills and low valleys; God over heaven, in heaven, and under heaven; and He has a mansion, *i.e.*, heaven, and the earth, and the sea, and all things that are in them. He inspireth all things. He quickeneth all things. He enkindleth all things. He giveth light to the sun, and to the moon. He created fountains in the dry land, and placed dry islands in the sea, and stars to minister to the greater lights. He hath a Son, coeternal and coequal with Himself; and the Son is not younger than the Father, nor is the Father older than the Son. And the Holy Ghost breatheth in them. And the Father, and the Son, and the Holy Ghost are not divided. I desire, moreover, to unite you to the Son of the heavenly king, for ye are daughters of an earthly king." And the daughters said, as if with one mouth and one heart, "How shall we come to believe in that king? Teach us duly, that we may see the Lord face to face—teach us, and we will do as you will say to us." Et dixit Patrici: "Do you believe that through baptism the sin of your mother and of your father shall be put away from you?" They answered, "We believe." "Do you believe in repentance after sin?" "Yes." And they were baptized. And Patrick blessed a white veil upon their heads; and they desired to see Christ face to face. And Patrick said to them: "You cannot see Christ except that you first taste death, and unless you receive the body of Christ and His blood." And the daughters replied, saying: "Give us the Communion, that we may be able to see the Prophesied One." And they after this received the Communion, and fell asleep in death, and Patrick placed them under covering, and in one bed [grave]; and their friends made a great lamentation over them. The druids then entered into conflict with Patrick, on account of the daughters having believed, and having gone to heaven, *i.e.*, Mael and Caplait. Caplait came crying against Patrick, for it was he [Caplait] who fostered the second daughter. Patrick preached to him, and he believed, and he cut off his hair. After this the other druid came, *i.e.*,

Tripartite Life of St. Patrick

Mael, and said to Patrick: "My brother has believed for thee," said he; "it shall not serve nor strengthen him," said he; "I will again lead him into paganism." And he was thus insulting Patrick; but Patrick preached to him, and the druid believed in God and Patrick. And Patrick shaved him; and hence "Mael is like Caplait" is a proverb; for it was together that they believed. And the day of weeping was finished, and the maidens were interred there; and Sen-Donahnagh of Magh-Ai was presented to Patrick for ever. And others say the relics of the maidens were brought to Ard-Macha, where they await the resurrection.

Patrick went afterwards to Tir-Caireda, and he founded a church at Ard-lice, *i.e.*, Sen-Domhnach, and he left Deacon Caeman in it. And Patrick erected Ard-Senlis, *ubi posuit Lalloc sanctam et tenuit locum in Campo Nento*; and they went with Bishop Cethech to his country. Of the race of Ailill was his mother; of Cenel-Sai [nigh] of Cinacht, from Domhnach-Sairigi at Damhliac-Cianain; and it was Bishop Cethech's custom to celebrate the great pasch in Domhnach-Sairigi; and in Ath-da-lorg, in Kells, he celebrated the little pasch, with Comgilla; for Cethech's people used to say that Comgilla was Cethech's servitor. Patrick went afterwards to the territory of Ui-Maine, and he left there an arch-priest (or deacon) of his people, *i.e.*, Deacon Juis, and he erected Fidharta; and Patrick left his books of orders and baptism with him; and he baptized the Ui-Maine; and Deacon Juis, in his old age, baptized Ciaran mac-int-sair, from Patrick's book, *quia CXL anni fuit quando Ciaran baptizavit, ut aiunt peritissimi.* Patrick's Franks, moreover, left him, viz., fifteen brothers and one sister, viz., Bernicius and Hibernicius, and Hernicus, etc., and Nitria, the sister. And many places were given to them. One of these is Imgoe of Baislic, between Hy-Maine and Magh-Nai. Patrick described to them the likeness of the place with his finger, from Cill-Garad, *quia venerunt ad Patricium ut obteret illis de locis quos invenerent.* Patrick also founded Cill-Garad, where Cethech [was left], and Ferta-gethich together. Then it was that Patrick made the well which is called Uarangarad, and he loved this water very much, *ut ipse dixit*:

"Uaran-gar—[Uaran-gar]—
O well! which I have loved, which loved me;
Alas! my cry, O dear God!
That my drink is not from the pure well."

Part II

Patrick went afterwards to Magh-Selcae, *i.e.*, to Dumha-Selca, where there were young men, the six sons of Brian, viz., Bolcderc, Derthacht, Echen, Cremthann, Caelcharna, Echuid; and Patrick wrote three names there in three stones, viz., *Jesus, Soter, Salvator*. Patrick blessed the Ui-Briuin from Dumha-Selca, and Patrick's seat is there between the stones *in quibus scripsit literas, et nona* (sic) *episcoporum cum illo illic fuerunt,* viz., Bronus of Caisel-Irra, Sachelus of Baislicmor in Ciarraighe, Brocaid of Imlech-ech (brother to Lomman of Athtruim), Bronachus, presbyter, Rodan, Cassan, Benen, comarb of Patrick, and Benen, brother of Cethech, Felartus, bishop, and his sister, a nun there, and another sister, *quae sit insola in mari Conmaicne, i.e.*, Croch-Cuile-Conmaicne. And he founded a church on Loch-Selca, *i.e.*, Domhnach-mor of Magh-Selca, *in quo baptizavit Ui-Briuin et benedixit*. Patrick went to Gregraidhe of Loch-Techet, and founded a church there in Drumma, and dug a well thereat, and no stream went into or came out of it, but it was always full, and its name is Bithlan (*i.e.*, ever full). He afterwards founded Cill-Atrachta in Gregraidhe, and [left] Talan's daughter in it, who received a veil from Patrick's hand. And he left a *teisc* and chalice with Atracht, the daughter of Talan, son of Cathbadh, of the Gregraidhe of Loch-Teched, sister of Caemhan of Airdne-Caemhain. Patrick blessed a veil on her head. Drummana was the name of the place in which they were; Machaire is its name to-day. A *casula* was sent down from heaven on Patrick's breast. "You shall have this *casula*, O nun!" said Patrick. "No," said she, "not to me was it given, but to thyself."

He then went to the sons of Erc; they carried off Patrick's horses, and Patrick cursed them, saying: "Your seed shall serve the seed of your brother for ever." Patrick went into Magh-Airtich, and blessed a place,;*i.e.*, Ailech-Airtigh, in Telach-na-cloch. And he went afterwards into Drummut of Ciarraighe-Airtigh, where he found two brothers fighting regarding the father's land after his death, *viz*, Bibar and Lochru, Tamanchend's two sons. Patrick stretched out his arms, and their hands became fixed to the swords, so that they were not able to lift or lower them, "Sit ye," said Patrick; and he blessed them, and made peace between them. And they gave the land to Patrick, for their father's soul. And Patrick founded a church there, where Conu the artifex is, the brother of Bishop Sechnall. Patrick went subsequently to Ciarraighe-Airne, where he met Ernaisc and his son Loarn under a tree, and Patrick wrote an alphabet for him, and stayed a week with them, with his twelve men. And Patrick founded a church there, *et tenuit ilium abbatem* (sic), *et fuit quidem spiritu sancto plenus.*

Tripartite Life of St. Patrick

And Patrick went to Tobar-Mucno, and advanced to Senchill *et fuit Secundinus solus sub ulmo frondosa separatim, et est signum crucis in eo loco usque in hunc diem.* And he afterwards went into the country of Conmaicne, into Cuil-Tolaigh, and he founded four-cornered churches in that place. One of these is Ard-Uscon, etc. He went to Magh-Cera, and stopped at Cuil-Corra, and founded a church in that place, *et baptizavit multos.*

Afterwards Patrick proceeded to Magh-Foimsen, where he met two brothers, viz., Luchtae and Derclam. Derclam sent his servant to kill Patrick, but Luchtse prevented him, to whom Patrick said: "There shall be priests and bishops of thy seed, and the race of thy brother shall be cursed, and shall be few." And he left in that place Cruimther-Conan, and went afterwards to Tobar-Stringle in the desert, and he was two Sundays [living] on that well.

Patrick went to the men of Umhall, to Achadh-Fobhair where Bishop Senach was ordained. The name Patrick conferred on him was "*Agnus Dei.*" And he it was who asked the three requests of Patrick—viz., that he should not oppose him as regards orders, that the place should not be called after him, and that what was wanting to complete his age should be added to the age of Mac Aenghusa. It was for him (Mac Aenghusa) that Patrick wrote an alphabet the day that Bishop Senach was ordained. Patrick desired truly to erect a *see* at Achadh-Fobhair, when he said: "I would remain here, on a small plot of land, after circumambulating churches and fastnesses; for I am infirm, I would not go." The angel said to Patrick:

> "Everything you select shall be yours—
> Every land, whether plain or rough,
> Both hills and churches,
> Both glens and woods,
> After circumambulating churches and fastnesses
> Though infirm, that you shall select."

Then Patrick left two trout alive in the well, and they will be there for ever, as he said:

> "The two inseparable trout,
> Which would advance against perpetual streams,
> Without obligation, without transgression—
> Angels will be along with them in it."

Part II

Patrick went to Cruachan-Aighle on the Saturday of Whitsuntide. The angel went to converse with him, and said to him: "God will not give thee what thou demandest; for He thinks the demands weighty and immense and great." "Is that His decision?" said Patrick. "It is," answered the angel. "This is my decision, then," said Patrick: "I shall not leave this Cruachan until I die or all the demands shall be given." Patrick was afterwards with illness of mind in Cruachan, without drink or food, from Shrove Saturday to Easter Saturday, just like Moses, son of Amra; for they were alike in many things. God accosted them both out of the fire; six score years was the age of each; the place of sepulture of both is uncertain. At the end of those forty nights and forty days the mountain around him was filled with black birds, so that he could see neither heaven nor earth. He sang cursing psalms at them, but they went not away from him. He then became angry with them; he rang his bell at them, so that the men of Erinn heard its sound. And he flung it at them, so that a gap was broken out of it, and that [bell] is Bernan-Brighte.

Patrick afterwards cried until his face and the front of his *casula* (cowl) were wet. No demon came after this to Erinn for the space of seven years, and seven months, and seven days, and seven nights.

The angel subsequently went to protect Patrick, and he cleaned his *casula*, and brought white birds about the Cruachan; and they used to chant sweet melodies for him. "I will bring so many souls from pain," said the angel, "and as many as would cover as far as your eye could reach on the sea." "That is no great boon for me," said Patrick; "not far can my eye reach over the sea." "You shall have between sea and land, then," added the angel. "Is there anything more granted to me besides that?" asked Patrick. "There is," said the angel; "you can bring seven every Saturday from the pains of hell for ever." "If anything be granted to me," observed Patrick, ["let me have] my twelve men." "You shall have it," said the angel; "and depart from Cruachan." "I shall not depart," said Patrick, "because I have been tormented, until I am recompensed. Is there anything else, then, to be granted to me?" asked Patrick. "Yes," said the angel; "you shall have seven every Thursday, and twelve every Saturday, from pains; and depart from Cruachan." "I will not depart," answered Patrick, "because I have been tormented, until I am recompensed. Is there anything else granted to me?" asked Patrick. "There is," answered the angel; "the great sea to come over Erinn seven years before the Judgment; and depart from the Cruachan."

Tripartite Life of St. Patrick

"I will not depart," said Patrick, "since I have been tormented, until I am gratified." "Is there anything more you demand?" asked the angel. "There is," answered Patrick; "that Saxons may not occupy Eriu, by consent or force, whilst I shall be in heaven." "It shall be granted thee," said the angel; "and depart from Cruachan." "I will not depart," said Patrick, "since I have been tormented, until I am gratified. Is there anything more granted to me?" asked Patrick. "There is," said the angel; "every one who repeats thy hymn from one day to the other shall not suffer pains." "The hymn is long and difficult," said Patrick. "Every one who repeats from *Crist illum*" (recte *Crist lim*, "Christ with me") "to the end, and every one who repeats the name, and every one who observes penitence in Eriu, their souls shall not go to hell; and depart from Cruachan" [said the angel].

"I will not depart," said Patrick, "for I have been tormented, until I am gratified. Is there anything more?" asked Patrick. "Yes," said the angel; "you shall have one man for every hair in your *casula* from pains on the Day of Judgment." "Which of the other saints who labor for God," said Patrick, "that would not bring that number to heaven? I shall not accept that," said Patrick.

"What will you accept, then?" asked the angel. "Here it is," said Patrick: "that I should bring from hell on the Day of Judgment seven persons for every hair in this *casula*." "It shall be granted to you," said the angel; "and depart from this Cruachan." "I will not depart," said Patrick, "for I have been tormented, until I am gratified." "Is there anything else you demand?" asked the angel. "There is," said Patrick: "the day that the twelve royal seats shall be on the Mount, and when the four rivers of fire shall be about the Mount, and when the three peoples shall be there—viz., the people of heaven, the people of earth, and the people of hell—that I myself may be judge over the men of Eriu on that day." "This thing cannot be obtained from the Lord," said the angel. "Unless this is obtained from Him, I will not consent to leave this Cruachan from this day for ever; and even after my death there shall be a caretaker from me there," answered Patrick.

The angel went to heaven. Patrick went to his offering. The angel came in the evening. "How now?" asked Patrick. "Thus," answered the angel: "all the creatures, visible and invisible, including the twelve apostles, entreated, and they have obtained. The Lord said that there came not, and would not come, after the apostles, a man more illustrious, were it not for the hardness of the request which is granted thee. Strike thy bell," said the angel; "thou art commanded from heaven to fall on thy knees, that it may be a blessing to the people of

Part II

all Eriu, both living and dead." "A blessing on the bountiful king that gave," said Patrick; "the Cruachan shall be left."

Patrick proceeded afterwards until he was in Achadhfobhair, where he celebrated the *ordo* at Easter. There are, moreover, "keepers" of Patrick's people in Eriu living still. There is a man from him in Cruachan-Aigle. The sound of his bell is heard, but it [the bell] is not found. And there is a man from him in Gulban-Guirt; and the third man from him is to the east of Cluain-Iraird, together with his wife. Both entertained Patrick in the reign of Laeghaire Mac Neill, and they are, and will be for ever, the same age. There is a man from him in Dromanna-Bregh; there is another man from him in Sliabh-Slainge—*i.e.*, Domangart, son of Eochaidh. It is he that will raise Patrick's relics a little before the Judgment. His cell is Rath-Murbhuilg, at the side of Sliabh-Slainge; and there is always a shin (of beef), with its accessories, and a pitcher of ale, before him every Easter, which is given to Mass people on Easter Monday always. Patrick's charioteer died, moreover, and was buried between Cruachan and the sea. Patrick went afterwards into the country of the Corco-Themne, and baptized many thousand persons there, and he founded four churches there, viz., in the three Tuagha.

Patrick went then to Tobar-Finnmaighe—*i.e.*, a well. It was told to Patrick that the pagans honored this well as a god. The well was four-cornered, and there was a four-cornered stone over its mouth, and the foolish people believed that a certain dead prophet made it, *bibliothecam sibi in aqua sub petra ut dealbaret ossa sua semper, quia timuit ignem, et zelavit Pat. de Deo vivo, dicens non vere dicitis quia rex aquarum fons erat hoc necnon cum eis habuit rex aquarum, et dixit Patricius petram elivari et non potuerunt elevavit autem eam petram; Cainnech, que, baptizavit Patricius, et dixit erit semen tuum benedictum in secula.* Cill-Tog, in the territory of Corco-Themne—it was this church that Bishop Cainnech, Patrick's monk, founded. One time, as Patrick was travelling in the plains of Mac-Ercae—*i.e.*, in Dichuil and Erchuil—he saw a large sepulchre there, viz., 120 feet in length. The brothers desiring that the dead man might be resuscitated, Patrick thereupon "awoke" the dead man who was in the sepulchre, and questioned him *quando, et quomodo, et quo genere, et quo nomine esset. Respondit sibi, dicens, "Ego sum Cass, filius of Glassi, qui fui subulcus Lugair Iruatae,* and Mac Conn's *fiann* killed me in the reign of Cairpre Niafer, in the hundredth year. I am here until to-day." Patrick baptized him, and he went again into his sepulchre.

Tripartite Life of St. Patrick

Quis comprehendere valet modi (sic) *diligentise orationis ejus omnes, namque psalmos, et ymnos et Apocalipsi, ac omnia cantica spiritualia scripturarum cotidie (quotidie) decantabat seu in uno loco seu in itinere gradiens.* From vespers on Sunday night until tierce on Monday Patrick would not come from the place where he might be.

One Sunday Patrick was in a cold, damp place, when great rain fell on the earth, but it rained not in the spot where Patrick was, *sicut in concha et vellere Gideoni accederat*. It was a custom with Patrick to place the cross of Christ over himself one hundred times each day and night; and he would go aside from his path, even though the cross were one thousand paces away, provided that he saw it or knew it to be in his vicinity; whether he was in a chariot or on a horse, he would proceed to each cross. One day Patrick omitted to visit a cross which was on his way, but he knew not that it was there. His charioteer said to him in the evening: "You left a cross which was on your way to-day without visiting." Patrick left his guest-house and his dinner, and went back to the cross. When Patrick was praying at the cross, "This is a sepulchre," said Patrick; "who was buried here?" A voice answered out of the sepulchre: "I am a poor pagan," it said, "and I was buried here; whilst living, I was injuring my soul until I died; and I was buried here afterwards." "What was the reason," asked Patrick, "that the sign of Christianity—*i.e.*, the cross—was placed over thy grave?" "This," answered the voice: "a certain woman that was in foreign lands, and her son was buried here in this country in her absence; and she came from foreign lands, and placed this cross over my grave. She thought it was over the grave of her son it was placed; for she was not able through grief to recognize her son's grave." "This is the reason that I missed the cross," said Patrick—"*i.e.*, its being over the grave of a pagan." The cross was afterwards raised by Patrick over the Christian's grave.

One time Patrick's charioteer wanted his horses; he could not find them, owing to the darkness of the night. Patrick lifted up his hand; his five fingers illuminated all the place as if they were five torches, and the horses were immediately found.

Patrick went across the Muaidh to Hy-Amhalghaidh; the twelve sons of Amhalgaidh, son of Fiachra, son of Eochaidh, came to meet him, viz., Aengus, Fergus, Fedhlimidh, Enna Crom, Enna Cullom, Connac, Cairbre, Echui Dianimh, Oena, Eoghan Coir, Dubchonall, Ailill of the rough face. The sons of Amhalghaidh were disputing about the sovereignty: twenty-four tribes (*i.e.*, old tribes) that were in the country; and they objected that they would not admit any man asking over them with an additional [nick] name. Aengus then imposed additional names upon his brothers. This Aengus was the proudest of Amhalghaidh's sons. Laeghaire, son of Niall, son of Eochaidh, King of Tara, and his brother Eoghan, son of Niall, decided the dispute. The sons of Amhalghaidh went to Tara in twelve chariots, *sicut in libris Patricii inventus, quod exirent in judicium tamen vii fratres de eis.* They were welcomed by the king at Tara. Aengus was foster-son to Laeghaire. He got a special welcome there. Aengus prayed the door-keepers that they would not admit Conall, the son of his brother—*i.e.*, the son of Enna Crom—into the fort; for Aengus feared his wisdom in arguing his right. Aengus obtained this request from the door-keepers. As Conall was outside the *lis*, he heard the sound of Patrick's bell from Tobar-Patrick at the fort. Conall went to him and saluted him. "O cleric!" said he, "do you know this expression which I have in commemoration—*i.e.*, '*Hibernenses omnes clamant ad te pueri,*' etc.—which two girls uttered in their mother's womb in our country?" "I am he whom that refers to," said Patrick; "and I heard it when I was in the islands of the Tyrrhene Sea, *et nescivi utrum in meam vel extra locuta sunt verba, et ibo tecum in regionem tuam baptizare, docere, evangelizare.*" Interrogat autem Patricius qua causa venit Conall, and Conall related the reason to Patrick, and he said that he was not allowed to enter Tara; to whom Patrick said: "Go in now, as the doors are open; and go to my faithful friend, Eoghan Mac Neill, who will assist you, if you lay hold, secretly, of the finger next his little finger, which is always a sign between us." And so it was done.

"Welcome," said Eoghan. "What is Patrick's wish?" Conall said: "That you assist me." Conall afterwards observed: "If it is according to youth precedence in a king's house or land is to be given, I am the youngest; if according to mother's age, Enna Cromm is the oldest." To which Laeghaire replied: "Honor to the senior, truly," said he, "and converse with the learned; but if jewels and treasures are given to any one, however, I will not deprive him of them." They came away, and Patrick with them, and Patrick gave his chariot to Conall, so that it was the thirteenth charlot. They went their way afterwards, and there was not good-will with Aengus for his brother's son and for Patrick. He told his two brothers—viz., Fergus and Fedhlimidh—to kill Patrick and Conall, as he had agreed on parting Laeghaire, after Laeghaire had instigated him thereto. They went northwards towards their country. The place which Aengus had fixed upon for the fratricide was in Corann. Fergus simulated sleep. His brothers refused what they had promised. "We will not kill the innocent," said they, "and will not commit murder upon our brother." Aengus went towards him (Patrick) to kill him, accompanied by two bands and two druids—viz., Reon and Rechred, of the race of Faelan the warrior. It is not more than a mile from the place whence Patrick saw the enemies, from the cross to the west of Cross-Patrick, to Cill-Forclann. Reon said that the ground would swallow Patrick on the place where he would see him. This was related to Patrick. "It is I who shall see him first," said Patrick. When Patrick saw him, the ground swallowed him up. "I will believe," said he, "if I am rescued." The ground flung him up until he was above the winds, and he fell down half alive. He believed, and was baptized. Rechred was also lifted up and let down until his head was broken against the rock, and fire from heaven burned him. The druid's rock is there. There is a church there. Cross-Patrick is its name, to the east of Coill-Fochlaidh. Telach-na-Druadh is the name of the place where the pagans were, to the west of Cross-Patrick. Glas-Conaigh is between them. Aengus said: "I will believe if my sister is resuscitated"—*i.e.*, Feidelm, daughter of Amhalgaidh, who died long before.

One time a blind man went to meet Patrick; he went in haste with the desire of being healed. One of Patrick's people laughed at him. "My *debroth*," said Patrick, "it would be fit that you were the blind person." The blind man was healed, and the hale was made blind, quod utrimque factum est. Mignae is the name of the person who was blinded; and he is the second man of Patrick's people who remained in Disert-Patrick, which is near the well at Cross-Patrick, and Donnmall was the other. Ruan, son of Cucnamha, Amhalgaidh's charioteer, that was healed there. Roi-Ruain is the name of the place where the blind was healed, and it belonged to Patrick afterwards. He met two *bacachs* in Ochtar-Caerthin. They complained to him of their infirmity, for they found it difficult to proceed through mountain or plain. What more shall I say? They were healed. He went to Domhnach-Mor, where Bishop Mucna is. He went afterwards to Cross-Patrick, where Aedh Fota, son of Eochaidh, son of Oengus, came to him; and he healed him from lameness at the fountain to the west of Cross-Patrick; and he (Aedh) presented to him a plot of land there, where he founded a residence, and he left two of his family there—viz., Teloc and Nemnall. Enna saw the druids (magi) wishing to kill Patrick, and he said to his son Conall, "Go and protect Patrick, that the *magi* may not kill him." Patrick perceived them, and ethereal fire burned them, to the number of nine.

Part II

He then founded Cill-Alaidh, and he left an illustrious man of his family there—*i.e.*, Bishop Muiredhach. Patrick baptized women—viz., Crebriu and Lesru, the two daughters of Glerann, son of Cummen. It was they that called upon Patrick from their mother's womb when he was in the islands of the Tyrrhene Sea. They are patronesses of Cill-Forglainn, in Hy-Amhalghaidh or Tirawley, to the west of Muaidh.

He went to Forrach-mac-Amalghaidh. Seven sons of Amalgaidh believed, including Enna and the king. It was then he baptized the pregnant woman and her offspring, and resuscitated another. Patrick and Conall went to the grave where the dead pregnant woman was, by the lower road to Cill-Alaidh. Aengus, however, went by the upper road. They reached the grave, and Patrick resuscitated the woman, and her son in her womb; and both were baptized in the well Aen-adharcae (from the little hillock of land that is near it the well was named). Being resuscitated, she preached to the multitudes of the pains of hell and the rewards of heaven, and with tears prayed her brother that he would believe for God and Patrick, which was done, and he was baptized. And in that day twelve thousand were baptized in the well of Aen-adharcae, ut dicitur: "On one day were baptized six great thousands, with the seven sons of Amhalgaidh. This was the number." Twelve thousand, truly, that believed for Patrick in Ui-Amhalghadha, and of those of Caille-Fochladh. And Patrick left Magister Manchen with them. He went southwards to the ford of Loch-Daela. The place was the property of Aengus. Patrick intended to found a residence for himself there. Aengus came quickly when he saw him (Patrick), for it was not from his heart that he believed when he was baptized and confessed the faith. "My *debroth*," said Patrick, "'twere right that thy houses should not be exalted, nor thy descendants after thee. Thy successors shall be seldom just, and there shall be fratricide through it."

He went to the east, to Lec-finn, where Patrick made the cross in the stone over Cill-mor-uachtair-Muaidh, to the west. But Lia-na-manach is its name at this day—*i.e.* Cruimther Monach's, or Olcan's church; but there was no church there at that time. And he baptized Eochaidh, son of Nathi, son of Fiachra, and resuscitated his wife Echtra, at Ath-Echtra, the little stream at the very door of Cill-mor. And Echtra's grave is on the margin of the ford. It is a sign of knowledge with them in their history to remember this grave. He (Patrick) sent Bishop Olcan to build where the church is to-day. Thus he came with an axe on his back, and Patrick told him that he should put up at the place where the axe would fall off his back; *quod factum est* where

Tripartite Life of St. Patrick

Cill-mor-uachtair-Muaidh is. He went afterwards to the north, to Lec-Balbeni, where he found and blessed the sons of Amhalgaidh; and he went out of the country from [the western] Bertlacha to the eastern Bertlacha, and passed it eastwards to the estuary of the Muaidh, towards the mouth of the sea. A young woman was drowned there before him; and he blessed the place, and said that no person should be drowned there for evermore. Patrick prophesied that the eastern Bertlacha should be with him, as it is in their history; and in the day of war the king of that region will be victorious, if true to Patrick. It was there, at the stream, the Gregraighe flung stones at Patrick and his people. "My *debroth*," said Patrick, "you shall be beaten in every conflict in which you may be; and you shall be subject to insult and contumely in every assembly in which you may be." "Arise, O Conall!" said Patrick, "that you may assume the *bachall*." Conall said, "If it please thee, I shall do so." "That shall not be," said Patrick; "but I will support thy valor, and will give comarbs to thy race, and thou shall be the Conall Sciath-bachall. The palm of laics and clerics shall be from thee; and every one of thy descendants in whose shield the sign of my *bachall* shall be will not be subdued."

All this Patrick did to him. He went eastwards into the territory of Hy-Fiachrach, by the sea. A water opposed his passage—*i.e.*, there was an unusually large rock in it—and he cursed it. On the water there is a place, Buaile-Patrick is its name—*i.e.*, a little mound—with a cross there, where Patrick rested a short time. Then the holy bishop, Bron of Caisel-Irra, and the holy Mac Rime of Cill-Corcaraidhe; and there he wrote an alphabet for him; and I have heard from another that in the said place he gave a tooth from his jaw to Bishop Bron, for he was dear to Patrick. Immediately on coming from the west, across the Muaidh, into Gregraighe, he met three virulent druids at Rath-Righbhaird, who were able to do nothing to him; and he said that there never would be wanting of this people a man of such magical knowledge.

Mac Erca, the son of Draighen, who is in Cill-roe-mor, in the territory of Hy-Amhalgadha. Patrick baptized the seven sons of Draighen, and he selected of them Mac Erca, and gave him to Bishop Bron to be fostered; for it would not be easy to take him far away, in consequence of the love of his father for him.

Patrick marked out the site of Caisel-Irra, and the flag on which Patrick's tooth fell is in the middle of the *lis*. Bishop Bron founded the place, and Patrick prophesied that the place would be deserted by Gentiles, *quod factum est*.

Part II

Then Patrick desired the fishermen to set their nets for him in the river—*i.e.*, in Sligech. They said to him, "A salmon is not taken in this period of the winter; but as you desire it, however," said the fishermen, "we will do so." They placed their nets, and caught large salmon; and they gave them to Patrick; and he blessed the river, so that Sligech is the most fruitful river of Erinn, for fish is caught in it every quarter (of the year).

Bishop Rodan, the herd—Patrick left him in Muirisk, in Cill-espuig-Rodain. His calves would only do what he counselled; wherefore the harpers and musicians had a proverb. The Callraighe of Cul-Cernadhan were in a secret place before Patrick, and they brought their spears close to their shields to assault Patrick and his people. "My *debroth*," said Patrick, "what you did is not good. Every battle and every conflict which you wage, and your children after you, will be gained over you." They forthwith knelt to Patrick, except five. Patrick said: "In any battle that may be won against you, though all Connacht be after you, no greater number than five shall fall of you." And so is it observed.

One time he was after going by Bernas-Ui-Oilella to go to Magh-Luirg, when he fell into water—*i.e.*, a river that goes into (*recte*, from) Loch-Techet. Ath-carpait is the name of the ford, near to Ess-mic-Eirc. Patrick cursed the eastern half of the water. "And the half from the ford westwards, why do you spare it?" asked his people. "A son of life will come who will set up there hereafter," said Patrick, "who will like fruitful water at his place"—*i.e.*, Colum-Cille, son of Fedhlimidh, at Ess-mic-Eirc. From the ford up to the lake the best fishing in Erinn is found there by all. From the ford down not much is taken there.

Patrick went afterwards into the territory of Magh-Luirg, when his horses were carried off by Cenel-Mic-Erca. And Patrick cursed the people of that country; but Bishop Maine of the Hy-Ailella, who prayed Patrick regarding forgiveness for his kinsmen, and Patrick modified the malediction. And Bishop Maine washed Patrick's feet with his hair and tears, and drove the horses into a meadow, and cleaned their hoofs in honor of Patrick. And Patrick said, "There shall be weeping, and wailing, and mourning with the inhabitants of that country; and there will not be neighborship there *in saecula saeculorum*"; *ut impletur*. And Patrick also said that a great part of that country should afterwards belong to him; which was fulfilled in the case of Nodain of Loch-Uama. Bishop Maine is also of Patrick's people, and Geintene in Echainech in Hy-Ailella.

Tripartite Life of St. Patrick

Patrick went after that into the territory of Callraidhe to Druim-dara, where Druim-lias is to-day. It was then he baptized Mac Caerthinn; and that place was presented to Patrick for ever. Patrick afterwards established himself on the offering in Druim-dara, Druim-lias to-day—*i.e.*, from Patrick's seats and from the sheds it was named. Patrick left his *dalta* Benen there in abbotship during the space of twenty years. He journeyed into the glens eastward, where Cenel-Muinremur is to-day. His two nostrils bled on the way. Patrick's flag [stone] (Lec-Patrick) is there, and Patrick's hazel (Coll-Patrick), a little distance to the west of the church. He put up there. Srath-Patrick it is named this day; Domhnach-Patrick was its former name. Patrick remained there one Sunday; *et haec est una ecclesia illius regionis*. Patrick went afterwards past Druim-cliabh, from Caisel-Irra, by the Rosses eastwards, along Magh-Eni, and founded Domhnach-mor of Magh-Eni. Then it was that he cursed the Dubh River for the refusal which the fishermen gave him. He blessed Drobhais, however, on account of the kindness which the little boys who were fishing there did to him.

Thrice Patrick went across the Shannon into the land of Connacht. Fifty bells, and fifty altar chalices, and fifty altar cloths he left in the land of Connacht, each of them in his church. Seven years was he preaching to the men of Connacht; and he left them a blessing, and bade them farewell.

Patrick went to Es-Ruaidh. He desired to establish himself there, where Disert-Patrick is, and Lec-Patrick. Cairbre opposed him, and sent two of his people, whose names were Carbacc and Cuangus, to seize his hands. "Not good is what you do," said Patrick; "if I were permitted to found a place here, the second to Rome of Letha, with its Tiber running through it, would be my establishment with its Es-Ruaidh through it; and your descendants would be comarbs in it." Cairbre declined then, as Patrick had foretold. Thereupon Cairbre incited a dog to attack Patrick. Cuangus struck the dog with a rod. Patrick said that Cairbre's race should not exceed a small band, and that the palm of laics or clerics would not be from him, *quod impletur*. But as to Cuangus, since he agreed to seize Patrick's hands for Cairbre, Patrick said that his race should not be more numerous than a company, and that illustrious men would be of them, *quod impletum est*. Cairbre promised to Cuangus, for seizing Patrick's hands, as much as he could see to the north of Sliabh-Cise. When he turned to take a view about him, a dark cloud closed around Cuangus, so that he only saw to the sea westwards, and to the *ash* eastwards. "This river, which

Part II

God gave you, Cairbre," said Patrick, "your share of it shall not be fruitful as regards fish" (*i.e.*, the northern half of the river in length was Cairbre's share—*i.e.*, the half next to Cenel-Conaill—for Crich-Conaill belonged to Cairbre at that time as far as Rath-Cunga); "but Conall's share (the southern half) will be fruitful"; *sic impletum est*, until Murghins, son of Maelduin, son of Scannal, an illustrious king of Cairbre's race, presented the unfruitful part to Colum-Cille; and it is now fruitful with Colum-Cille.

He (Patrick) went afterwards between Es-Ruaidh and the sea into Crich-Conaill, where Rath-Chunga is at this day. He fixed a stake there, and said that it would be an abode and establishment for seven bishops; and there Bite is now, the brother's son of Aisicus from Elphin.

It was then also that he foretold of Domhnall, son of Aedh, son of Ainmire—viz., he fixed a pole in Ard-fothaidh, and on the morrow it was bent; and Patrick said that the place would be the seat of a king, which was fulfilled in Domhnall. On Sith-Aedha Patrick blessed Conall Mac Neill, when Patrick's hands would fall on the head of Fergus. Conall wondered at this thing, when Patrick said:

> "A youth (*i.e.*, Colum-Cille) shall be born of his tribe,
> Who will be a sage, a prophet, and poet,
> A glorious, bright, clear light,
> Who will not utter falsehood."

After Patrick had blessed the Cenel-Conaill, and had left a blessing on their forts and rivers and churches, he went into the country of Eoghan, the son of Niall, across Bernas of Tir-Aedha into Magh-Itha, and to Domhnachmor of Magh-Itha, where he left Dudubae, son of Corcan, of his people. And Patrick said to his people: "Take care that you meet not with the lion, Eoghan, son of Niall." Muiredhach, the son of Eoghan, who was in the front of the youths, met on the way Sechnall, who was in the rear of the host of clerics. Sechnall said to Muiredhach: "You would have a reward from me, if you would persuade your father to believe." "What reward?" asked he. "The sovereignty of thy tribe shall for ever belong to thy heirs," said Sechnall. "I will," answered Muiredhach. In Fidhmor it was that Eoghan met with Patrick, where the flag (*lec*) is. "If you would believe in your country," said Patrick, "the hostages of the Gaedhil would come to you."

Tripartite Life of St. Patrick

"I am not good-looking," said Eoghan; "my brother precedes me on account of my ugliness." "What form do you desire?" asked Patrick. "The form of the young man who is under (*i.e., who is bearing*) your satchel—*i.e.*, Rioc of Inis-bo-finde," said Eoghan. Patrick covered them over with the same garment, the hands of each being clasped round the other. They slept thus, and afterwards awoke in the same form, with the difference of the tonsure. "I don't like my height," said Eoghan. "What size do you desire to be?" asked Patrick. Eoghan reached up his hand with his sword. "I should like this height," said he; and he immediately grew to that height. Patrick afterwards blessed Eoghan, with his sons. "Which of your sons is dearest to you?" asked Patrick. "Muiredhach," said he. "Sovereignty from him for ever," said Patrick. "And next to him?" asked Patrick. "Fergus," answered he. "Dignity from him," said Patrick. "And after him?" asked Patrick. "Eocha Bindech," said Eoghan. "Warriors from him," said Patrick. "And after him?" asked Patrick. "They are all alike to me," answered Eoghan. "They shall have united love," said Patrick.

Patrick went to Ailech of the kings, when he blessed the fort and left his flag there; and he prophesied that kingship and pre-eminence should be over Erinn from Ailech. "When you lift your foot out of your bed to approach it, and your successor after you," said Patrick, "the men of Erinn shall tremble before you."

He blessed the whole island (Inis-Eoghain) from Belach-ratha; and he gave a blessing of valor to Eoghan. Then it was that Patrick said:

> "My blessing on the *tuatha* (territories)
> I give from Belach-ratha,
> On you, you descendants of Eoghan,
> Until the day of judgment.

> "Whilst plains are under crops,
> The palm of battle shall be on their men.
> The armies of Fail (Ireland) shall not be over your plains;
> You shall attack every *telach* (tribe).

> "The race of Eoghan, son of Niall,
> Bless, O fair Brigid!
> Provided they do good,
> Government shall be from them for ever.

"The blessing of us both
Upon Eoghan Mac Neill,
On all who may be born from him,
Provided they are obedient."

Eochaidh, son of Fiachra, son of Eoghan, was baptized with Eoghan, and Patrick's covenant was made between them; and whosoever transgresses it shall not have children born to him, and his body will not rot in the clay.

Where Patrick went after this was into Daigurt in Magh-Dula. He built seven Domhnachs (churches) about Fochaine (*i.e.*, *flumen*), namely, Domhnach-Dola, Domhnach-Seinlis, Domhnach-Dara, Domhnach-Senchua, Domhnach-Minchluane, Domhnach-Catte, Both-Domhnaigh.

Patrick proceeded into Tir-Eoghain of the Islands—namely, into the territory governed by Fergus—and he took to build a *disert* at a certain place; Achadh-Driman was the proper name of the land in which he built it. But Coelbhadh, son of Eoghan, drove him from thence, and Patrick said that in consequence thereof his race should never have a goodly house there. *Quod probatum est super* by Comman, son of Algasach, of the race of Coelbhadh, who was at Eas-nac-Eire, who made a house there, but, before he had the roof on it, it was broken down by a young cleric of the family of Domhnach-mor-Maighe Tochair.

"Thou shalt receive welcome from me," said Aedh, son of Fergus. There is neither bank nor wall between him and the aforesaid, and it was there that he erected Domhnach-mor-Maighe-Tochair, *ribi XL, dubas mansit et Mac Cairthin reliquit*.

Patrick proceeded from Domhnach-mor-Maighe-Tochair into Bredach, and there he met the three Deachans, the sons of Patrick's sister, in the country of Ailell, son of Eoghan, and he ordained Oengus, the son of Ailell, in that place, and he remained there on Sunday; Domhnach-Bile is its name.

When Patrick was at Ailech-Airtich in Sonnacht, in Cinel-Enda, Enda came to him. *"Da mihi hunc locum,"* said Patrick. *"Quasi non babussemus clericos,"* said Enda. On the morrow *venit Enda et suus filius secum*, Echu Caech. Patrick had turned off to pray, and his people to baptize, to confer orders, and to propagate the faith. The two Maccairthinns were there at the time, namely, *qui est at Clochar et qui est at Domhnach-mor-Maighe-Tochair*. "Confer ye the degree of bishop upon my son," said Enda. "Let Patrick be consulted," said Patrick's champion, Maccairthinn of Clochar. "It is our duty," said the other; "I will confer the order." When Patrick, he said, "Ye have conferred orders in my absence on the son of the Wolf; there shall be strife in the church of the one for ever; there shall be poverty in the church of the other." *Quod impletur*: strife at Clochar; Domhnach-mor-Maighe-Tochair, poverty is there. "The son upon whom the degree was conferred, two persons, after committing murder, shall profane his relics. One hundred and twenty years until a son shall be born in the southern parts [who shall reconsecrate his church], and it shall be restored to me again." *Quod totum impletum est.* The first place where his relics were was a high and beautiful spot, but they were carried thence after a short time to a lower place; and the first place where they were is deserted, and robbers and murderers are accustomed to dwell there, through Patrick's curse. And his church was ceded to Ciaran Mac-an-tsair, but was restored to Patrick again. This Echu, son of Enda, is at this day called Bishop Echan.

As Patrick was in Tir-Enda-Airtich at Tulach-liag, in Leitir, he stuck [wattles for] a church there, which afterwards became a bush. After this he went to the Lei, on the east of the Bann, *ubi non capiebant homines pieces nisi in nocte usque ad illud tempus. Deinde imperavit eis Patricius ut in die caperent, et sic erit in finem seculi.*

Patrick went afterwards into Dal-Araidhe and Dal-Riada. Then he proceeded to Ror to Carn-Setna, southwards, where he heard the screams of an infant from out of the ground. The carn was demolished, the sepulchre was laid bare, and a smell of wine arose around them out of the sepulchre. They saw the living child with the dead mother. A woman that died of ague; she was brought across the sea to Eriu, and the child was born after death; and seven days, it is said, it lived in the tumulus. "That is bad (*olc*)," said the king. "That shall be his name (*Olcan*)" said the druid. Patrick baptized him; and he is Bishop Olcan, of the community of Airther-Maighe, in the district of Dal-Riada. And Mac Nisse; of Condere, read his psalms with Patrick....

Patrick received welcome in the district from Erc's twelve sons. And Fergus Mor Mac Erca said to Patrick: "If I am preferred before my brothers in the division of our land, I will offer some to you." And Patrick gave to Bishop Olcan this part—*i.e.*, Airther-Maighe. Patrick said to Fergus: "Though thy esteem with thy brothers is not great to-day, it is thou that shall be king. The kings of this land and of Fortren shall be from thee for ever"; and this is what was fulfilled in Aedan Mac Gabhrain, who possessed Alba by force. Patrick left many cells and establishments in the territory of Dal-Riada.

Part II

He founded Fothraidh, and left two of his people in it—viz., Presbyter Cathbadh, and the monk Dimman; and he founded Rath-Mudhain, and left Presbyter Erclach in it; he left Bishop Nem in Telach-Ceniul-Aenghusa; Dachen-nindan in Domhnach-Cainri, in Cothraighe; Enan in Druim-Indich; and Bishop Fiachra in Cuil-Echirainn. And Patrick blessed Dun-Sobhairce; and Patrick's well is there, and he left a blessing upon it.

He went afterwards to Dal-Araidhe. He found Caelbadh's twelve sons before him. He proposed to found a place where Cill-glas is. He was repelled from it; and it belongs to him yet; and he left two of his people there—viz., Glaisiuc and Presbyter Libur. And he determined that he would found a place where Lathrach-Patraic is. It is there Daniel, Patrick's angel and dwarf, is. It is there Patrick's well is—*Slan* is its name—which Patrick discovered there. Saran, the son of Caelbad, seized his hand to expel him; and Patrick took heaven and land from him. Connia, the son of Caelbadh, however, received Patrick with humility, and gave him Domhnach-Combair; and Patrick blessed him, and declared that kings and chieftains should be of his race for ever. And he founded many churches in Dal-Araidhe—viz., Domhnach-mor of Magh-Damhairne, and Rath-Sithe (and he left two of his people there), and Telach-Conadain, and Gluaire in Latharna (and Mac Laisre is in it). He founded Glenn-indechta, and Imlech-[c]luana, in Semhne (where Caemhan was left), and Rath-Escuip-Indich, in the territory of Ui-Erca-chein.

After some time the aforesaid Saran bore off some men in captivity from the district of Dal-Riada. Bishop Olcan met him, and the poor people were grievously complaining to him. Olcan interceded, but it was of no avail, unless he would assure heaven to Saran. "I cannot do so, indeed," said he, "for Patrick has deprived thee of it." "I will kill thy people about thee but thee alone," said he, "and I will slay all these captives; and wherever I shall find a priest (*tailcend*), I shall bring him under the edge of the sword."

Whereupon Bishop Olcan promised him heaven. He came afterwards from the north to offer submission to Patrick. It was reported to Patrick that Bishop Olcan had promised baptism and heaven to the person to whom he had denied them. They met to the north of Cluain-Fiachna, on the way, going different directions. "The chariot over him," said Patrick. "It is not allowable," said the charioteer, "that it should go over a bishop." He told him (Bishop Olcan) that his establishment on earth would not be high, and that it would be thrice destroyed; as was afterwards fulfilled, for it was ruined by Scandal,

King of Dal-Araidhe, and by Cucuaran, and by fire also. "Laech-dich, son of Bresal, and his land, shall belong to the young boy bearing the satchel," said Patrick, "one of thy own people—*i.e.*, Mac Nisse of Condere—and to one not born yet—*i.e.*, Senan of Inis-Altich. Thy merit in heaven will be illustrious."

Saran's guilt it was that was here laid upon Bishop Olcan. Saran's brother, Nadsluagh, was submissive to Patrick; and he was in captivity on Patrick's arrival. "You shall have from me," said he, "the site of your *regles*." "Where will you give it me?" asked Patrick. "On the brink of the Bann, in the west," said Nadsluagh, "where the boys are burning the *ratha* (ferns)." "It shall be mine, truly," said Patrick; "a descendant of mine and thine shall be there"—*i.e.*, Bishop Coirpre, son of Deggell, son of Nadsluagh; it is he that is in Cul-rathain, on the eastern brink of the Bann. Bishop Brugach, who is in Ratha-Maighe-Aenaigh, in Crich-Conaill, it was that conferred orders on Bishop Coirpre. Patrick, also, it was that conferred orders on Bishop Brugach; so that he (Bishop Coirpre) is a descendant of Patrick in this wise. Patrick gave no malediction to any of the twelve sons of Caelbad, except to the king alone—*i.e.*, Saran. It was he that had acted disobediently to him. It was on this occasion that Patrick brought with him Bishop Guasacht, son of Milchu, from the territory of Dal-Araidhe; it was he whom Patrick left in Granard, and the two Emirs also, Milchu's two daughters; it is they that are in Cluam-Bronaigh, ut diximus.

The way Patrick went was into the territory of Dal-Araidhe, across Fertais-Tuama, to Ui-Tuirtre. He was forty nights in Finnobair, and determined to build a city there for its suitability—Loch-Nechach being on one side of it, and Sliabh-Calland on the other. Cairthen Mor, king of the country, went to him, and ordered him off. He (Patrick) deprived him and his children of the sovereignty. Patrick afterwards gave the sovereignty to Cairthend Beg, who was in exile from his brother; and Patrick baptized him, and blessed his wife and the being that was in her womb. "My *debroth*," said Patrick, "the being that is in thy womb shall be full of the grace of God; and it is I that twill bless a veil upon her head." The woman was Mogan, daughter of Fergus Mor Mac Nissi, King of Dal-Riada; and Trea, daughter of Cairthend, was the daughter who was in her womb; and it was Patrick who blessed a veil on her head, as he prophesied. The angels, moreover, that brought the veil from heaven, and placed it on her head, down over her eyes; and Patrick began to raise it up. "Why is it not good to leave it as it was placed?" asked Trea. "It is good indeed," answered Patrick. She never saw anything during her life except what she saw through that veil.

Patrick had seven Domhnachs in Ui-Tuirtre—viz., Domhnach-Fainre, Domhnach-Riascad, Domhnach-Fothirbe, Domhnach-Righduinn, Domhnach-Brain, Domhnach-Maelain, Domhnach-Libuir.

Where Patrick went afterwards was to Feara-Gabrae, and they were not obedient to him. Patrick said that they would go afterwards with tribute to his church in winter-time, and that extern tribes would get their country; *quod impletum est*. Patrick went afterwards to Fera-Imchlair, and he baptized and blessed them; and he left with them Cruimther Colum, and Patrick's book of orations, and his bell therewith; they are miraculous things unto this day.

When Patrick concluded his triumphant career in the present life, as the Apostle Paul said, "I have fought the good fight; I have finished my course; I have kept the faith; as to the rest, there is laid up for me a crown of justice, which the Lord the just judge will render to me in that day," he received communion and sacrifice from Bishop Tassach. His remains and relics are here regarded with honor and veneration by the earthly church. Though great his honor and veneration on the earth, greater still will they be in the Day of Judgment, when the fruit of his preaching will be committed to him as to each other high apostle, with the apostles and disciples of Jesus, in the union of the nine choirs of angels, in the union of the Divinity and the Humanity of the Son of God, in the unity which is nobler than all unity—in the unity of the Holy Trinity, Father, Son, and Holy Spirit. I beseech mercy through the intercession of Patrick. We ask that we may all ourselves obtain this union *in saecula saeculorum*. Amen.

[It should be observed that, at the commencement of each of the three parts of the Tripartite Life, there are several pages of Latin, which were intended by the author as a sort of introduction or preface to what follows in each part. They are made up principally of Scriptural quotations strung loosely together. These quotations have general reference to the establishment of Christ's kingdom upon earth, and are obviously intended to bear upon the happy introduction of Christianity into Ireland through the labors of our glorious apostle. At the end of each of the parts, in like manner, are some paragraphs, by way of peroration, devoted chiefly to the praises of the great saint, who dedicated the greater part of an unusually long life to the service of God, by the regeneration of our pagan ancestors. The language of both prefaces and perorations, whether corrupted by the copyists in transcription, or originally so written, is a most barbarous Latin. For the reasons indicated it has been deemed better to omit the pages alluded to, merely giving a few words of the commencement of each. In the Irish original, also, as was usual in early Irish manuscripts, there are a considerable number of Latin quotations or sentences, which in some cases have been translated, and in others given as they stood, without any attempt to correct the style.]

PART III.

Mirabilis Deus in sanctis suis. Spiritus Sanctus, à quo omne donum, et gratiarum charismata utrique, et novi et veteris Testamenti Ecclesias, data, haec protulit per os Regii Psalmistae Davidis filii, etc.

Patrick left Presbyter Conaedh in Domnach-Airther-Maighe, in the territory of Hy-Briuin of the north. He rested there on Sunday, and then went after Patrick from that place as far eastwards as the wood. "What brought you?" asked Patrick. "I cannot bear your absence, holy man," said he. "No wonder," observed Patrick; "the place around thee is not the place of a son of life, but a place for pig-eaters; the soil of the place shall never be reddened" (which we have proved when Connacan, son of Colman, son of Niall Frossach, went into the district with an army, nine men moved off from a tree which Artifex, a pilgrim, selected. He was beheaded; eight were liberated, however, in his land).

Patrick went afterwards to Telach-Maine, and received a welcome from Maine, son of Conlaedh, who humbled himself to him; and Patrick blessed him, and blessed his wife, so that she was fruitful, and brought forth two daughters. Patrick baptized them, and blessed veils on their heads, and left a senior with them to instruct them.

Patrick did not visit Ard-Macha on that occasion, but went into the territory of Hy-Cremthand, where he founded churches and residences. One time, as Patrick was coming from Clochar, from the north, his strong man—*i.e.*, Bishop Mac Carthend—carried him across a difficult place; and after lifting up Patrick, he said: "Uch, uch." "My *debroth*," said Patrick, "you were not accustomed to say that word." "I am old and infirm," said Bishop Mac Carthend, "and you have left all my early companions in churches, whilst I am still on the road." "I will leave thee in a church," said Patrick, "that shall not be too near us for familiarity, that shall not be too distant for intercourse between us." And Patrick afterwards left Bishop Mac Carthend in Clochar, and the

Domhnach-Airgid with him, which was sent to Patrick from heaven when he was on the sea coming to Erinn.

Patrick went after that to Lemhuin. Finnabhair is the name of the hill on which Patrick preached. Three days and three nights was he at the preaching, and each day did not seem to them longer than one hour. Then it was that Brigid slept at the preaching, and Patrick did not allow her to be awakened. Patrick asked her afterwards what she had seen. She said: "I saw fair synods and white oxen and fair cornfields; behind them spotted oxen, and black oxen after these. I afterwards saw sheep and pigs, and dogs and wolves, fighting amongst themselves. I saw subsequently two stones, one little and the other big. A drop was shed on each of them. The little stone increased at the 'drop,' and silvery sparks burst from it. The large stone withered, moreover." "They were the two sons of Eochaidh, son of Crimthann," said Patrick. Cairpre Damhairgit believed, and Patrick blessed him, and blessed his seed. Bresal, moreover, refused, and Patrick cursed him. Patrick also explained the whole vision of Brigid in an admirable manner.

He resuscitated Eochaidh, son of Crimthann, from death. Eochaidh possessed a daughter—*i.e.*, Cinnu—whom her father wished to marry to a man of noble family—*i.e.*, to the son of Cormac, son of Cairpre Mac Neill; she, walking along, met Patrick with his companions on the way. Patrick preached to her that she unite herself to the spiritual prophet; and she believed, and Patrick instructed her, and baptized her, afterwards. When her father was subsequently seeking for her, to give her to her man, she and Patrick went to converse with him. Patrick requested that he would permit her to wed the Eternal Spouse; Eochaidh agreed to this, if heaven would be given to him therefor, and he himself not be compelled to be baptized. Patrick then promised these two conditions, though he thought it hard. The king afterwards consented that his daughter—*i.e.*, Cinnu—should be united to Christ, and Patrick made her a female disciple to him, and commanded a certain virgin to instruct her *i.e.*, Cechtumbar of Druim-Dubhain, in which place both virgins rest.

After many years, moreover, the aforesaid Eochaidh reached the end of his life; and when his friends would remain by him, he said: "Let me not be buried," said he, "until Patrick comes." And when Eochaidh finished these words, his spirit departed. Patrick, moreover, was at this time in Ulster, at Sabhall-Patrick; and the death of Eochaidh was manifested to him, and he decided on going to Clochar-mac-Daimhin, where he found Eochaidh, who had been inanimate twenty-four hours. When Patrick went into the house where the body was, he sent out the persons who were about the body. He bent his knees to the Lord, and shed tears; and he prayed, and said in a clear voice: "Rise, O King Eochaidh! in the name of Almighty God"; and immediately, at the voice of the servant of God, he arose. When he had composed himself, he spoke, and the grief and lamentations of the people were changed to joy. And forthwith Patrick instructed the king in the rule of faith, and baptized him. He also commanded him, before the people, that he would describe the pains of the impious and the joy of the saints, and that he would speak to the people, that they might believe all that is said of the pains of hell and the joys of the blest to be true. And he spoke of these things, as he was commanded. And Patrick offered him a choice—*i.e.* fifteen years in the chief kingship of his country, if he would live piously and truthfully, or to go to heaven, if he preferred it. But the king said: "Though the sovereignty of the entire globe were given to me, and though I might live for many years, I would count it all as nothing in comparison with the good shown to me. Hence it is that I pray more and more that I may be freed from the miseries of the present life, and sent to the eternal joys exhibited to me." To whom Patrick said, "Go in peace, and journey to the Lord." Echu (or Eochaidh) gave thanks to God in the presence of his people, and he commended his soul to the Lord and Patrick, and his spirit departed to heaven.

Where Patrick went afterwards was to the territory of Ui-Meith-Tire, to Tech-Thalain; and he left Bishop Cilline there, and other holy men of his people, and the relics of saints which he brought with him across the sea from the east. Then it was that three robbers of Ui-Meith-Tire carried off the second goat that was wont to be bringing water, and they came to swear falsely to Patrick respecting him, but the goat cried from the bodies of the three who had acted treacherously. "My *debroth*," said Patrick, "the goat himself announces you as thieves. From this day forth goats shall stick to your children and kindred"; which has been fulfilled.

Eoghan, son of Brian, son of Muiredach, son of Imchadh, son of Colla-fo-Crich, was King of Ui-Meith when the people believed, and he (Patrick) blessed them. Eoghan besought Patrick to resuscitate his grandfather, *i.e.*, Muiredach. Patrick afterwards resuscitated him, and buried him again in the Erende, on the borders of Mughorna and Ui-Meith; but the place belongs to Mughorna. Then Patrick went into the district of Mughorna, to Domhnach-Maighen especially. When Victor, who was in that place, heard that Patrick had come to it, Victor went, to avoid Patrick, from the residence to a thorny brake at the side of the town. God performed a prodigy for Patrick. He lighted up the brake in the dark night, so that everything therein was visible. Victor went afterwards to Patrick, and gave him his submission; and Patrick gave him the church, and imposed the degree of bishop on Victor, and left him in Domhnach-Maighen. And Patrick blessed Mudhorna, and said that the most illustrious of laics and clerics should be of them. And he bade farewell to them, and left a blessing with them. Afterwards Patrick went to Fera-Ros, to Enach-Conglais, where he remained a Sunday. There it was that the Ui-Lilaigh gave the poison to Patrick in the lumps of curds. Patrick blessed the pieces, and made stones of them.

When Patrick went on Monday across the ford southwards, the Ui-Lilaigh went with fifty horsemen upon the ford after him to slay him. Patrick turned towards them upon the bank to the south of the ford, and he raised his left hand, and said: "You shall neither come out of the ford here nor go the other way; but you shall be in that water for ever." The water immediately went over them. Ath-O'Lilaigh is the name of the ford for ever, and the stone lumps are at Enach-Conglaise, in commemoration of the miracle, to this present day.

He afterwards went to Rath-Cuile, where he blessed the Fera-Cuile—*i.e.*, the Ui-Seghain. He went to Bile-Tortan after that, and constructed a church for Presbyter Justin near Bile-Tortan, which is near the community of Ard-Breccan. When Patrick was journeying to the territory of Leinster from Domhnach-Tortan, he remained a night at Drum-Urchaille. Patrick went afterwards to Naas. The site of his tent is in the green of the fort, to the east of the road, and his well is to the north of the fort (*dún*), where he baptized Dunlaing's two sons, Ailill and Illann, and where he baptized Ailill's two daughters, Moghain and Feidelm. And their father dedicated them to God and Patrick, from their consecrated virginity, and he (Patrick) blessed the veil on their heads.

Messengers went from Patrick to call the steward of the fort of Naas—*i.e.*, Fallen. He avoided Patrick; and he pretended to be asleep, through enmity and ridicule of Patrick. And Patrick was told that the steward was asleep. "My *debroth*," said Patrick, "I should not be surprised if it were his last sleep." His people went to awake him, and they found him dead, through the disobedience he showed to Patrick. And hence is the proverb amongst the Irish: "Fallen's sleep in the fort of Naas."

Dricriu was the King of Ui-Garchon at Patrick's coming, and the daughter of Laeghaire Mac Neill was his wife. And he refused Patrick regarding his feast at Rath-Inbhir, on Laeghaire's account. But Cilline gave him welcome, and killed his own cow for him, and gave to Patrick the quantity of flour that he brought for his support from the king's house, whereupon he (Patrick) prophesied that Cilline's son should be king of Ui-Garchon.

He went afterwards to Magh-Life, and founded cells and houses there; and he left Usail in Cill-Usaille, and Iserninus and Mac Tail in Cella-Cuilinn, and other saints. On his going into Western Life, the sons of Laighis prepared water-pits in the way before him, and a covering over them. "For God's sake," said the little boys, "drive on your horses." "Drive on, then, for God's sake, your horses," said Patrick. But no injury was done to them; and he cursed Laighis (*i.e.*, Laighis, son of Find) where Moin-Choluim is to-day; and Patrick said that there would be neither a king nor a bishop from them, and that a foreign lord should be over them for ever.

Brig, the daughter of Fergnad, son of Cobtach, of the Ui-Ercain, went to report to Patrick the enmity that was in store for him. Patrick blessed her, and her father, and her brothers, and the Ui-Ercain altogether, and he said that they would never be without distinguished laics and clerics of them.

Then Patrick alighted on the hillock which was then called Bile-Mac-Cruaich; to-day, however, it is called Forrach-Patrick; and he said that there would never be a foreign king or steward over them; and when the King of Leinster would be distributing the feast in his royal house, he would have one shin (of beef), and the King of Ui-Ercan the other; they should have Patrick's respect, Patrick's *forrach* (seat), the dignity of laics and clerics, wealth, and immortality. Eight princes they had up to the reign of Conchobhar, son of Donnchadh, in Tara. Laighis, moreover, was the tribe-name of the youths who committed the misdeed; and neither king nor bishop shall be from them, but strange lords shall govern them, and they shall never have rest from persecution and complaints.

Patrick went from Tara until he met Dubhtach Mac Ui-Lugair at Domhnach-mór of Magh-Criathar, in Ui-Cinnse-laigh, who believed for Patrick. Patrick requested from him a handsome youth who would not be of low family—a man of one wife, for whom but one son was born. "Hem," said Dubhtach, "that is Fiacc, son of Ere, I am afraid—the man of those qualities, who went from me to the territory of Connacht with poems for the kings." At these words he (Fiacc) came. "What are you considering?" asked Fiacc. "Dubhtach for the crozier," said Patrick. "That will be a blemish to many, indeed," said Fiacc;

"why should not I be taken in place of him?" "You will be received, indeed," said Patrick. He was tonsured, baptized, an alphabet was written for him, and he read his psalms in one day, as has been related to me. He was ordained in the grade of bishop, and the bishopric of Leinster was given to him by Patrick; and his only son, Fiachra, was also ordained. This Fiacc was, therefore, the first bishop ordained in Leinster. Patrick gave Fiacc a case—viz., a bell, a reliquary, a crozier, and a book-satchel; and he left seven of his people with him—viz., Mochatoc of Inis-Fail, Augustin of Inis-Bec, Tecan, and Diarmait, and Nainnid, Paul, and Fedilmidh.

He (Fiacc) afterwards resided in Domnach-Feic, and he was there until threescore of his people died with him. Then the angel went to him, and said to him: "It is on the west of the river (Barrow) thy (place of) resurrection is, in Cul-maighe"; and he said that where they would meet a boar, there they should build their refectory; but where they would meet a hind, there they should place the church. Fiacc said to the angel that he would not go until Patrick would come to mark out the boundary of his place, and to consecrate it, and that he might get the place from him. Patrick went then to Fiacc, and marked out his place with him, and fixed his site. And Crimthan presented that place to Patrick, for it was Patrick that baptized him; and it is in Sleibhte he is buried. It was there, afterwards, Fiacc was ordained.

They (the Ui-Ercan) were at that time persecuted by the King of Leinster, Crimthann, son of Enna Ceinnselach, so that they went into exile. Of them are the *manachs* in Hy-Crimthann, and the *manachs* in Ulster, and Cenel-Enna in Munster. Of them is Fiacc, of whom we have spoken before. Fiacc, Aengus, Ailill Mar, Conall, and Etirscel were five brothers. Their father was the son of Ere.

Through the action of Patrick, the king granted him (Fiacc) land, the fifth part of his father's possessions, and thereon it was that he built Sleibhte.

The Aengus in question afterwards killed the king, Crimthann, son of Enna Ceinnselach, to avenge his exile. In thirties and forties are the churches which he gave to Patrick in the east of Leinster, and in Ui-Cennselaigh, including Domnach-mor of Magh-Criathar and Inis-Fail, where Mochonoc and Mochatoc are, and Erdit and Augustin in the smaller island (but their shrines are in Sleibhte, since the place was occupied by Gentiles); Domnach-mór of Magh-Reta. Patrick was a Sunday here (*i.e.*, in Domnach-mór of Magh-Reta), and they were on that Sunday building Rath-Baccain, the royal fort of the district. Patrick sent to prevent this, but no notice was taken thereof. Patrick said,

Part III

"Its building shall be troublesome, unless 'offering' is done there every day." He also said that the fort would not be inhabited until the wind (*gaeth*) would come from the lower part of hell. This was Gaithini, son of Cinaed, who rebuilt the fort in the time of Fedhlimidh, and of Conchobhar in Tara.

After that Patrick had founded churches and establishments in Leinster, moreover, he left a blessing upon Ui-Cennselaigh, and upon the Leinstermen all; and he afterwards ordained Fiacc Find in Sleibhte, as bishop of the province.

He then went along Bealach-Gabhran, into the district of Ossory, and founded churches and establishments there; and he said that distinguished laics and clerics should be of them, and that no province should have command over them, whilst they remained obedient to Patrick. Patrick took leave of them afterwards, and he left the relics of holy men with them, and some of his people, in the place where Martar-tech is this day in Magh-Roighne. At Druim-Conchind, in Mairge, the cross-beam of Patrick's chariot broke when he was going to Munster. He made another of the wood of the *druim*. It broke immediately. He made one again, and it broke also. Patrick said that there should never be any implement made of the timber of that wood, which has been fulfilled, for even a pin is not made of it. Patrick's Disert is there, but it is waste.

Patrick went afterwards to the territory of Munster, to Cashel of the Kings. When Aengus, son of Nadfraech, got up in the morning, all their idols were prostrate; and Patrick and his people came to the side of the fort, and he (Aengus) bade them welcome, and took them into the fort to the place where Lee-Patrick is to-day. And Patrick after that baptized the sons of Nedfraech, and the men of Munster besides, and left a blessing and prosperity upon them. And he blessed the fort—*i.e.*, Cashel—and said that only one race should be there for ever. And he was seven years in Munster. The learned calculate that he made an offering on every seventh ridge that he traversed in Munster.

When Patrick was baptizing Aengus, the point of the crozier went through Aengus's foot. Patrick asked, "Why was it that you did not tell me?" "Because," said he, "I thought it was the rule of the faith." "You shall have its reward," said Patrick; "your successors from this day forth shall not die of wounds." No one is King of Cashel until Patrick's comarb ordains him and imposes the grade on him. Patrick said:

"The sons of Nadfraech, of sounding fame,
Of them shall be kings and chieftains;
Aengus, from the lands of Feimhen,
And Ailill, his brother."

And twenty-eight kings, of the race of Ailill and Aengus, reigned in Cashel, ordained with the crozier, until the time of Cenngegan.

Patrick went after this to Muscraidhe-Breogain, and founded churches and establishments there.

One day he was washing his hands at a ford there, when a tooth fell out of his mouth into the ford. Patrick went upon the hillock to the north of the ford; and persons went from him to look for the tooth, and forthwith the tooth glistened in the ford like a sun; and Athfiaclai is the name of the ford, and Cill-fiacia is the name of the church where Patrick left the tooth and four of his people—viz., Cuircthe and Loscan, Cailech and Bedan. He bade them (*i.e.*, the Muscraidhe) farewell, and left them a blessing.

He went afterwards to Aradha-Cliach until he was in Iochtar-Cuillenn in Ui-Cuanach; and Ailill, son of Cathbadh, son of Lughaidh, of the Eoghanacht of Airther-Cliach, met him. His wife went on the hillock where they (the clerics) were, and said: "The pigs have eaten our son Ailill through savageness," said she. And Ailill said: "I will believe if you resuscitate my son for me." Patrick commanded the boy's bones to be collected, and he directed a Céle-Dé of his people—*i.e.*, Malach Britt—to resuscitate him. "I will not offend the Lord," said he. (He was seized with doubt.) Patrick said: "That is pitiful, O Malach! thy house on earth shall not be high; thy house shall be the house of one man." His house is in the northeastern angle of the southern Deise; its name is Cill-Malaich. Five persons can never be supported there.

Patrick afterwards commanded Bishops Ibar and Ailbhe to resuscitate the boy; and he prayed the Lord with them. The boy was afterwards resuscitated through Patrick's prayers. The boy subsequently preached to the hosts and multitudes in Patrick's presence. Ailill and his wife thereupon believed; and all the Ui-Cuanach believed, and were baptized in that place. And the seat of the four—*i.e.*, of Patrick, Ailbhe, Bishop Ibar, and the young boy—is in the place where the boy was resuscitated. His father said: "God cures by the hand of the physician." Four persons stole Patrick's horses southwards. Patrick forgave it. One of them was a leech, whose name was

Part III

Caencomhrac; another was a carpenter; another was a bondman; but the fourth was a groom, whose name was Aedh. Patrick called the latter, and blessed his hands, and told him that his name should be Lamaedh from that day; and from him are the Lamhraighe.

It was then that disease seized Ailill's wife, who was *enciente*, so that death was nigh unto her. Patrick asked what was the matter. The woman answered: "An herb I saw in the air, and I saw not the like of it on the earth; and I shall die, or the being in my womb shall die, or we shall both die, unless I taste that herb." Patrick asked her of what kind was the herb. "Like rushes," said the woman. Patrick thereupon blessed rushes, so that they were apparently the same. The woman then ate them, and was forthwith whole; and after some time she gave birth to a son, and blessed Patrick; and it is reported that Patrick said that all women who should eat of this herb would be healed.

He desired to remain by the side of Clar, at the fort of Coirpre and Brocan, but he was not permitted; and Patrick said that there never would be a king or bishop of the race of Colman, who opposed him. He also said that the place would belong to himself afterwards, and left a man of his people there, after a long period—*i.e.*, Caemhan of Cill-Rath.

Ibar then selected a place of residence in Grian, in Aradha-Cliach. Dola opposed him. Patrick said that there would not be a house of his (Dola's) there, or, if there should be, it would be only for (the lives of) two or three. This was fulfilled. They (Dola's descendants) removed to Airther-Cliach, and Dal-Modola is their name until this day.

Nena went to him (Patrick), who refused to receive him, and said that he would not be prosperous. No successors of his occupied the place there since, but they are enslaved by Muscraighe-Mittine. "Menraighe" they are called.

As Patrick was leaving this place, the women of Grian came to bewail his departure from them. Patrick blessed them, and said that the children they would bear to extern tribes would be illustrious.

Patrick was in Aradha-Cliach, at Tedil (the name of a hill). When he was bidding farewell, two of his people remained behind. They were sent for, and found asleep under a bush there. This was told to Patrick. "Here their resurrection will be," said he; which is true. Muin and Lomchu [who are] in Cill-Tidil [were left there] by Patrick.

He went after this to Hy-Fidhgente, where Lonan, son of Mac Eire, provided a banquet for him. Mullach-Cae, over against Carn-Feradhaigh on the south; and a man of Patrick's people was preparing

Tripartite Life of St. Patrick

the banquet along with the king—*i.e.*, Deacon Mantan. A band of artists came up to Patrick to solicit food, and would have no excuse. "Go to Lonan and to Deacon Mantan, that they may relieve me," said Patrick. Who answered, "No, until our banquet is blessed." Then Patrick said:

> "The youth who comes from the north,
> To him is vouchsafed the triumph;
> To Cothraige he comes,
> With his little wether on his back."

At that very time came another youth, attended by his mother, carrying on her back a cooked wether to the king's supper. Patrick begged of him to give him the wether to save his honor. The son at once gave it cheerfully, though the mother was unwilling to do so, through fear of the king. Patrick gave the food to the players; and immediately the earth swallowed them. Derc, son of Scirire, of the southern Desi, was their chief; and Patrick said there would not be a king, or heir apparent, or bishop of his family of Lonan for ever; and he assured Mantan, the deacon, that his church would not be exalted on earth, but should be the abode of the dregs of the people, and that swine and sheep would trample on his own remains; but to Nessan, who had saved his honor, he promised that he should be honored among the nations. And he baptized him, ordained him deacon, and founded for him a church—*i.e.*, Mungarit. His mother excused herself, and he said she should not be buried in her son's church. This came to pass, for her grave is to the west of Mungarit, and the bell of the great church is not heard in that place; they are almost together, only separated by a wall.

The men of North Munster, to the north of Luimnech, went in fleets of boats to meet Patrick southwards as far as Domhnach-mor of Magh-Aine—*i.e.*, to Dun-Nocfene, then and now so called; and he baptized them in Tir-glass, to the southeast of it. He afterwards went to Finnine, to the northwest of Domhnach-mor, a hill from which he could see the country to the north of Luimnech, when he gave a blessing to the men of North Munster, who had gone with a profusion of gifts to meet Patrick.

Cairthend, son of Blat, the senior of the Clann-Toirdhelbhaigh, believed in the Lord, and Patrick baptized him at Sangul (*i.e.*, a different angel that went to converse with him that day, and not Victor). No children were born to Cairthenn, except deformities, up to that

Part III

time. It was then that Eochu Ballderg was born to Cairthenn. Patrick that procured this; and he formed a clot of gore, which was on his (Eochu's) body, as a sign of that miracle. Patrick himself did not go into the country, but he saw from him about Luimnech to the west and to the north; and he blessed the district and its islands, and prophesied of the saints who would appear in them, of their names, and the time in which they would come. "The green island in the west," said Patrick, "in the mouth of the sea; the lamp of the people of God shall come into it, who will be the head of counsel to this district—*i.e.*, Senan of Inis-Cathaigh—six score years from this." (Senan, son of Gerrgenn, son of Dubhthach.) He did not go across Luachair, indeed, into West Munster. He prophesied of Brenainn, son of Ua-Altae, who was to be born 120 years after, which was fulfilled.

Patrick then went into the southern Desi, and set about building a church in Ard Patrick; and Lec-Patrick (Patrick's flag [stone]) is there, and the limits of his church. Derball, son of Aedh, opposed him. Derball said to Patrick: "If you would remove that mountain there, so that I could see Loch-Lunga across it to the south, in Fera-Maighe-Feine, I would believe." Cenn-Abhrat is the name of the mountain, and Belach-Legtha (melted pass) is the name of the pass which was melted there. When the mountain began to dissolve, Derball said that whatever he (Patrick) did would be of no use. Patrick said to Derball: "There shall be no king nor bishop of your family, and it will be allowable to the men of Munster to plunder you all every seventh year for ever as bare as a leek."

As Patrick was in the district of the Desi, awaiting the king of the country—*i.e.*, Fergair, son of Rossa—Patrick said to him, after his arrival: "How slowly you come!" "The country is rough" [said he]. "True indeed," said Patrick. "There shall be no king from you for ever. What delayed you to-day?" asked Patrick. "The rain delayed us," said the king. "Your meetings shall be showery for ever," said Patrick. Patrick's well is there, and also the church of Mac Clairidh, one of Patrick's people. And assemblies are not held by the Desi except at night, because Patrick left that sentence upon them, for it was towards night they went to him. Patrick then cursed the streams of that place, because his books were drowned in them, and the fishermen gave his people a refusal. Patrick said that they would not be fruitful, and that there would never be any mills upon them, except the mills of strangers, notwithstanding their great profusion up to that time. He blessed the Suir, moreover, and the country around; and it is fruitful in fish, except the places where those streams (*glaise*) flow into it.

Tripartite Life of St. Patrick

Patrick went into Muscraighe-thire, and to preach and plant the faith there. He met three brothers of that nation, men of power—Furic and Muinnech and Mechar, the sons of Forat, son of Conla. Muinnech believed at once, and Patrick baptized and blessed him, and said that illustrious heroes and clerics should descend from him for ever; and that the chief kingship of his country should be [filled up] from him for ever, as the poet said:

"Muinnech the Great believes
In Patrick, before all;
That there might be over his country
Chieftains of his race for ever.

"Mechair believed,
For he was a true, just man.
Patrick gave him a lasting blessing—
The companionship of a king.

"Fuirec, the furious man,
Opposed, though he was hoary and old;
His ultimate fate, after this world,
Is not to be deplored.

"When Cothraige imposed
A tribute (*cain*) upon noble Eri,
On the host of this island
He conferred a lasting blessing.

"Choice was this blessing
Which he conferred seven-fold
On each one who would observe
His plain rule, his law.

"Whoever would disobey
The noble, just rule,
Should not see him, he said,
In the region of the saints.

"Patrick's *cain* in great Munster
Was imposed on each family,

Until Dungalach violated it,
[Who was] of the race of Failbhe Flann.

"Dungalach, son of Faelghus,
Grandson of just Nadfraech,
Was the first who transgressed
Patrick's *cain* from the beginning.

"It is related in histories,
All ages know it,
That his successorship is not found
In Cashel of the Kings.

"There is not of his progeny
(Though he won battles)
A noble bishop or herenagh,
A prince or a sage.

"Saergus the Young, also—
* * * * *
Violated the *cain* he had adopted,
For the vehement Dungalach.

"It is seen that illustrious men
Are not of his wondrous family;
If there are now, they will not
Be found till judgment comes."

Now, after that Patrick had founded cells and churches in Munster, and had ordained persons for every grade, and healed all sick persons, and resuscitated the dead, he bade them farewell, and left his blessing with them. He then went to Brosnacha, and the men of Munster followed after him, as if with one accord; and their households (hillocks? *telcha*) followed them, to go after Patrick. Patrick thereupon blessed the households (hillocks?), and they remained in their places.

Where the men of Munster overtook Patrick, men, youths, and women, was at Brosnacha, when they raised great shouts of joy at seeing him; hence it is called Brosnacha. It was here Patrick resuscitated Fot, son of Derad, a Munsterman, who had been twenty-seven years dead. It was here, too, he blessed the banquet of the youth at Craibhecha, with Bishop Trian, a pilgrim of the Romans, by which the men of Munster were satisfied, and the saints of Eri besides. He again bade farewell to the men of Munster, and gave them his blessing, saying:

> "A blessing on the men of Munaani
> Men, sons, women.
> A blessing on the land
> That gives them food.
> A blessing on all treasures
> Produced upon the plains.
> A blessing upon Munster.
> A blessing on their woods
> And on their sloping plains.
> A blessing on their glens.
> A blessing on their hills.
> As the sands of the seas under ships—
> So numerous be their homesteads,
> In slopes, in plains,
> In mountains, in peaks,
>   A blessing."

Patrick afterwards went to the territory of Hy-Failge, and Foilge Berrad boasted that, if he met Patrick, he would kill him, in revenge of the idol Cenn Cruach; for it was this that was a god to Foilge. This boast of Foilge was kept back from Patrick by his people. One day Odran, his charioteer, said to Patrick: "Since I have been a long time driving for you, O Patrick! let me take the chief seat for this day. Be you the charioteer, O father!" Patrick did so. After this Foilge came, who dealt a thrust through Odran, in the guise of Patrick. "My curse," said Patrick. "Upon the tree of Bridam," said Odran. "Be it so," replied Patrick. Foilge died at once, and went to hell. As to Foilge Ross, indeed, it is his children who are in the district at this day; and Patrick blessed him, and from him is the sovereignty of the district filled for ever.

On one occasion, as Patrick was going the way of Midluachair, in order to come to Uladh, he met carpenters cutting down trunks of yew. Patrick saw their blood ooze from their palms in the operation. "Whence are ye?" said Patrick. "We are slaves belonging to Trian, son of Fiac, son of Amalgad—*i.e.*, brother to Trichem—who are in subjection and affliction, so much so that we are not allowed to sharpen our axes (irons), in order that our work may be the heavier and more difficult, so that blood flows from our hands." Patrick blessed the

Part III

irons, so that they could easily cut with them; and he went to the king, to Trian's fort. Patrick fasts on him. He disobeyed. He returns on the morrow from the fort. He spat on the rock which was there on his way, so that it broke into three pieces; one third part was cast to a distance of one thousand paces. Patrick said: "Two-thirds of the fast on the rock, another third on the fort and king, and on the district. There will not be a king nor *roydamhna* of the children of Trian. He shall die prematurely himself, and shall go down to a bitter hell." The wife of the king came, following Patrick. She performed penance, and knelt. Patrick blessed her womb and the beings in it—*i.e.*, Setna, son of Trian, and Iarlaid, son of Trian. Sechnall that baptized Setna, Patrick that baptized Iarlaid, and Patrick said that he would be his successor afterwards. Trian himself proceeded to bind and maltreat the slaves who reported him. His horses bore him off in the chariot, and his driver, so that they went into the lake. Loch-Trena is its name. This was his last fall. He will not arise out of the lake till the vespers of judgment; and it will not be to happiness even then. There was a certain wicked man in the country of Uladh—*i.e.*, Magh-Inis—at that time, an impious man, and a son of death—*i.e.*, Mac Cuill—who was plundering and killing the people. On one occasion Patrick and his companions passed by him a certain day, and he desired to kill Patrick. This is what he (Mac Cuill) said to his followers: "Behold the *tailcenn* and false prophet, who is deceiving every one; let us arise and make an attack on him, to see if perhaps his God will assist him." This is what they planned afterwards: to bring one of their people on a bier, as if dead, to be resuscitated by Patrick, and to deceive Patrick; and they threw a cover over his body and over his face. "Cure," said they to Patrick, "our companion for us, and beseech your God to awake him from death." "My *debroth*," said Patrick, "I would not wonder if he were dead." Garban was the name of the man; and it is of him Patrick said: "The covering of Garban shall be the covering of a dead body; but I shall tell you more: it is Garban who will be under it." His friends removed the covering from his face, so that they found it so. They afterwards became mute, and then said: "Truly this is a man of God." They all believed at once. Mac Cuill believed also; and he went on sea in a cot of one hide, by the command of Patrick. Garban was awakened from death through the prayers of Patrick. Mac Cuill, however, went that very day on sea, and his right hand towards Magh-Inis, until he reached Manann; and he found two venerable persons before him on the island. It was they who preached the word of God in Manann, and it is through their teaching that the people of that island were baptized and believed; their names are Coninnri and Romael. When those men saw Mac Cuill in his cot, they took him off the sea; they received him kindly; and he learned the divine knowledge with them, and spent his whole time with them, until he got the episcopacy of the place after them. This is Mac Cuill, of Mann, famous bishop and abbot. May his holy favor assist us!

One time Patrick slept on a Sunday, on a hill over the sea, at Drombo, when he heard the noise of Gentiles digging a rath on the Sabbath. He called them, and told them to cease. They heeded him not, but began to mock him. And Patrick said: "My *debroth*, your labor shall not profit you." This was fulfilled; for on the following night a great tempest arose and destroyed their work, according to the word of Patrick.

Patrick said to Eochaidh, son of Muiredach that there should never be a king from him, nor enough of his race to constitute an assembly or army in Ulster, but that his tribe would be scattered and dispersed, that his own life would be short, and that he would meet a tragic fate. This was the cause Patrick had against Eochaidh, as the learned say: Two virgins, who had offered their virginity to the Lord, he bound and sent on the waves to be drowned, as they refused to adore idols and to marry. When Patrick heard this, he besought the king regarding them, but in vain. "Your brother Cairell has got thy luck, since he granted me a good request," said Patrick, "and you have lost it through your disobedience. He (Cairell) shall be a king, and there shall be kings and chiefs of his race over your children and over all Ulster"; so that of him sprang the race of kings, and of his son Deman, son of Cairell, son of Muiredhach, according to the words of Patrick. Eochaidh's wife cast herself at the feet of Patrick. He baptized her, and blessed the child in her womb—*i.e.*, the excellent and illustrious son, Domangart, the son of Eochaidh. He it was whom Patrick left in his body, and he will be there for ever. He turned back to the Fera-Ross, and commenced a church in Druim-Mor, in the territory of Ross, over Cluain-Cain. It was here the angel went to him and said: "It is not here you have been destined to stay." "Where shall I go?" said Patrick. "Pass on to Macha northwards," said the angel. "The *cluain* below is fairer," replied Patrick. "Be its name Cluain-Cain" (*fair cluain*), answered the angel. "A pilgrim of the Britons shall come and occupy there, and it shall be yours afterwards." "*Deo gratias ago*," said Patrick. Where Patrick went then was to Ard-Phadraig, on the east of Lughmadh, and he proposed to build an establishment there. The Dal-Runter went after him to keep him, as one presented him to another.

Part III

He blessed them afterwards, and prophesied that distinguished chiefs and clerics should be of them, and that they should have possessions outside their territory, because they went forth out of their own country after him. Patrick used to come every day from the east, from Ard-Phadraig, and Mochta used to come from the west, from Lughmadh, that they might converse together every day at Leac-Moctae. One day the angel placed an epistle between them. Patrick read the epistle, and what was in it was: "Mochta, the devoted, the believing, let him be in the place he has taken." Patrick goes, by the order of his king, to smooth Macha, and he assigned the twelve lepers left in Ard-Phadraig to Mochta, and their food used to be given to them each night by Mochta. Patrick went afterwards to the *macha*, by order of the angel, to a place where Rath-Daire is this day. There was a certain prosperous and venerable person there. Daire was his name—*i.e.*, Daire, son of Finchad, son of Eogan, son of Niallan. Patrick asked for a site for his *regles* from him. Daire answered: "What place do you desire?" "In this great hillock below," says Patrick, where Ardmacha is to-day. "I will not give it," said Daire, "but I will give you a site for your *regles* in the strong rath below," where the *ferta* are to-day. Patrick founded a church there, and remained a long time. One day two steeds of Daire's were brought to him, to his *regles*, for the *relig* was grassy. Patrick became very angry. The horses died at once. His servant told this to Daire, saying: "That Christian," said he, "killed your steeds, because they ate the grass that was in his *regles*." Daire was angry at this, and ordered his servants to plunder the cleric, and expel him from his place—*i.e.*, the *ferta*. A colic seized on Daire immediately, so that death was near him. His wife recalled the plunder of Patrick, and told Daire that the cause of his death was the attack on Patrick. She sent messengers to beg prayer-water for Daire from Patrick. Patrick said: "Only for what the woman has done, there would never be any resurrection from death for Daire." Patrick blessed the water, and gave it to the servants, with orders to have it sprinkled over the horses and over Daire. They did so, and immediately they all returned from death. A brazen caldron was brought to Patrick as an offering from Daire. "*Deo gratias*," said Patrick. Daire asked his servants what Patrick said. They answered, "*Gratzicum*." "This is little reward for a good offering and a good caldron," said Daire. He ordered his cauldron to be brought to him. "*Deo gratias*," said Patrick. Daire asked what Patrick said when they were bringing the caldron from him. The servants answered: "It was the same thing he said when we were bringing it away from him—*Gratzicum*." "This is a good word with them, this *Gratzicum*," said Daire; "*Gratzicum* when giving it to him, and *Gratzicum* when taking it away from him." Daire and his wife then went with his submission to Patrick, and gave Patrick the caldron willingly back again, and the hill which he before asked; and Patrick accepted and blessed them, and founded a church in that place called Ard-Macha. Patrick and his divines, and Daire, with the nobles of Airther besides, came to the hill to mark out its boundaries, and to bless it, and consecrate it. They found a doe, with its fawn, in the place where the Sabhall is to-day, and his people went to kill it. *Prohibuit Patricius, et dixit, "Serviat sibi postea,"* and sent it out of the hill northward, to the place where Telac-na-licce is to-day, *ibi magna mirabilia fecit.*

Daire's daughter loved the person Benen; sweet to her was the sound of his voice in chanting. Disease seized her, so that she died of it. Benen carried *cretra* to her from Patrick, and she suddenly afterwards arose alive, and loved him spiritually. She is Ercnait, the daughter of Daire, who is in Tamlaght-bo.

One time there came nine daughters of the King of the Longbards and the daughter of the King of Britain on a pilgrimage to Patrick; they stopped at the east side of Ard-Macha, where Coll-na-ningean is to-day. There came messengers from them to Patrick to know if they should proceed to him. Patrick said to the messengers that three of the maidens would go to heaven, and in that place (*i.e.*, Coll-na-ningean) their sepulchre is. "And let the other maidens go to Druim-fenneda, and let one of them proceed as far as that hill in the east." And so it was done.

Cruimthir went afterwards, and occupied Cengobd; and Benen used to carry fragments of food to her every night from Patrick. And Patrick planted an apple-tree in Achadh-na-elti, which he took from the fort, in the north of the place—*i.e.*, Cengoba; and hence the place is called Abhall-Patrick, in Cengoba. It was the milk of this doe, moreover, that used to be given to the lap-dog that was near the maiden—*i.e.*, Cruimthir.

Another time, when Patrick was at rest in the end of night, at Tiprad-Cernai, in Tir-Tipraid, the angel went to him and awoke him. Patrick said to him: "Is there anything in which I have offended God, or is His anger upon me?" "No," said the angel; "and you are informed from God," added the angel, "if it is it you desire, that there shall be no share for any else in Eriu, but for you alone. And the extent of the termon of your see from God is to Droma-Bregh, and to Sliabh-Mis, and to Bri-Airghi." Patrick replied: "My *debroth*, truly," said Patrick, "sons of life will come after me, and I wish they may have honor from

God in the country after me." The angel responded: "That is manifest. And God gave all Eriu to you," said the angel, "and every noble that will be in Eriu shall belong to you." "*Deo gratias*," said Patrick.

Patrick was enraged against his sister—*i.e.*, Lupait—for committing the sin of adultery, so that she was pregnant in consequence. When Patrick came into the church from the eastern side, Lupait went to meet him, until she prostrated herself before the chariot, in the place where the cross is in Both-Archall. "The chariot over her," said Patrick. The chariot passed over her thrice, for she used still to come in front of it; so that where she went to heaven was at the Ferta; and she was buried by Patrick, and her *ecnaire* (requiem) was sung. Colman, grandson of Ailill, of the Ui-Bresail, that fixed his attention on Lupait at Imduail. Aedan, son of Colman, saint of Inis-Lothair, was the son of Lupait and Colman. Lupait implored of Patrick that he would not take away heaven from Colman with his progeny. Patrick did not take it away; but he said they would be sickly. Of the children of this Colman, moreover, are the Ui-Faelain and Ui-Dubhdara.

One time Patrick's people were cutting corn in Trian-Conchobhair. They were seized with great thirst, whereupon a vessel of whey was taken to them from Patrick, who persuaded them to observe abstinence from tierce to vesper time. It happened that one of them died; and he was the first man that was buried by Patrick—*i.e.*, Colman Itadach, at the cross by the door of Patrick's house. What Patrick said when it was told to him was: "My *debroth*, there will be abundance of food and ale and prosperity in this city after us."

Once the angels went, and took from off the road the stone which was before the chariot, and its name is Lec-na-naingel. It was from that place—*i.e.*, from Druim-Chaile—that Patrick with his two hands blessed the *macha*. The way in which Patrick measured the rath—*i.e.*, the angel before him, and Patrick behind, with his people, and with the holy men of Eriu, and the Bachall Isa in Patrick's hand. And he said that great would be the crime of any one who would transgress in it, as the reward would be great of such as fulfilled the will of God in it.

The way in which Patrick measured the *ferta* was thus, viz., one hundred and forty feet in the *lis*, and twenty feet in the great house, and seventeen feet in the kitchen, and seven feet in the chamber; and it was thus he always constructed the establishment.

The angel went to Patrick in Ard-Macha. "This day," said he, "the relics of the apostles are distributed in Rome throughout the four parts of the globe; and it would be becoming in you that you should go

Tripartite Life of St. Patrick

there." And the angel bore Patrick in the air. At the southern cross, in Aenach-Macha, it was that four chariots were brought to Patrick; at the northern cross, moreover, it was that God manifested to him the form he will have in the Day of Judgment. And he went in one day to Comur-tri-nuisce. He left Sechnall in the episcopacy with the men of Eriu until the ship would come which would bear him from the shore of Letha.

Patrick went subsequently, and arrived at Rome; and sleep came over the inhabitants of Rome, so that Patrick brought away a sufficiency of the relics. These relics were afterwards taken to Ard-Macha with the consent of God and with the consent of the men of Eriu.

What was brought were the relics of three hundred and sixty-five martyrs, and the relics of Peter and Paul, and Lawrence, and Stephen, and of many more; and a cloth in which was the blood of Christ and the hair of the Virgin Mary. Patrick left this collection in Armagh, according to the will of God, of the angel, and of the men of Eriu.

His relics—the relics of Letha—were stolen from Patrick. Messengers went from him to the Abbot of Rome. They brought an epistle from him, directing that they should watch the relics with lamps and torches by night for ever, and with Mass and psalmody by day, and prayers by night, and that they should elevate them every year (for multitudes desired to see them).

Two brothers of the Ulstermen, Dubhan and Dubhaedh, stole Patrick's two garrons from the land (*tir*) to the east of the Nemhed (Tir-suidhe-Patrick is its name). They carried them off into the moor to the south. Dubhan said; "I will not take what belongs to the *tailcenn*." "I will take what comes to me," said Dubhaedh. Dubhan went and did penance. "Your comrade's journey is not a good one," said Patrick. He got a fall, so that his head was broken, and he died. Dubhan became a disciple, and was ordained; and Patrick said: "Here thy resurrection shall be." Another time, in carrying a bag of wheat from Setna, son of Dallan, to Patrick, the manna which dropped from heaven, in a desert place, over Druim-mic-Ublae, Patrick's horse [fell] under it. A grain of the wheat dropped out of the bag, and the horse could not rise until there came from Patrick. "This is the reason," said Patrick through prophecy, "a grain of wheat that fell out of the sack, in the spot where the cross is on the way southwards to the Nemhed." "Nenihed then will be the name of the place where the horse stopped," said Patrick; and so it is.

Part III

Another time Sechnall went to Armagh, and Patrick was not there. He saw before him two of Patrick's horses unyoked, and he said: "It were fitter to send those horses to the bishop—*i.e.*, to Fiacc." When Patrick returned, this thing was told to him. The chariot was attached to the horses; and he sent them on without a man with them until they were in the disert with Mochta. They went right-hand-wise on the morrow to Domhnach-Sechnaill. They then went eastwardly to Cill-Auxili. They went afterwards to Cill-monach; then, after that, to Fiacc to Sleibhte. The reason for giving the chariot to Fiacc was because he used to go every Whit-Saturday as far as the hill of Druim-Coblai, where he had a cave. Five cakes with him, as report says. On Easter-Saturday he used to come to Sleibhte, and used to bring with him a bit of his five cakes. The cause of giving the chariot to Fiacc was that a chafer had gnawed his leg, so that death was nigh unto him.

Sechnall said to Patrick: "When shall I make a hymn of praise for thee?" "You are not required," observed Patrick. "I have not said to thee, 'Shall it be done?'" said Sechnall, "for it will be done, truly." "My *debroth*," said Patrick, "it is time it were finished now"; for Patrick knew that it would not be long until Sechnall's time [arrived], for he was the first bishop who went under the clay of Eriu.

When he was composing the hymn, they were holding an assembly near him. It was commanded to them from him that they should go away from the place. They began to mock him. He told them that the ground would swallow them; and it swallowed twelve chariots of them at once. Sechnall said to Patrick's people at Ferta-Marta: "A good man is Patrick, but for one thing." When he heard these words with his people, he asked Sechnall for the previous message, and Sechnall said; "O my lord! the reason I have said it is because little do you preach of charity." "Young man," said Patrick, "it is for charity that I preach not charity; for if I did preach it, I would not leave a stud of two chariot horses to any of the saints, present or future, in this island; for all belong to me and them."

Sechnall went with his hymn to Patrick, and Patrick went along Belach-Midhluachra into the territory of Conaille. He returned along the mountain westwards. He met Sechnall. They saluted one another. "I should like that you would hear a [hymn of] praise which I have made for a certain man of God," said Sechnall. "The praise of the people of God is welcome," answered Patrick. Sechnall thereupon began "*Beata Christi custodit,*" fearing that Patrick would prohibit him at once if he heard his name. When he sang "*Maximus namque,*" Patrick arose. The place where he sang so far is called Elda. "Wait," said

Sechnall, "until we reach a secret place which is near us; it is there the remainder will be recited." Patrick enquired on the way how "*Maximus in regno coelorum*" could be said of a man. Sechnall replied: "It [*maximus*] is put for the positive [*magnus*]," or because he excelled the men of his race of the Britons or Scoti. They came then to a place called Dal-Muine, where he, Patrick, prayed and sat; and Sechnall afterwards sang the remainder of the hymn; and Patrick heard his name, and thereupon thanked him. Three pieces of cheese, and butter, were brought up to him from a religious couple—viz., Berach and Brig. "Here is for the young men," said the woman. "Good," said Patrick. A druid came there, whose name was Gall-drui ("foreign druid"), who said: "I will believe in you if you convert the pieces of cheese into stones"; which God performed through Patrick. "Again convert them into cheese"; and he did. "Convert them into stones again"; and he did. "Convert them again." Patrick said: "No, but they will be as they are, in commemoration, until the servant of God, who is Dicuill of the Ernaidhe, shall come here." The druid (*magus*) believed.

Patrick flung his little bell under a dense bush there. A birch grew through its handle. This it was that Dicuill found, the *betechan*, Patrick's bell—a little iron bell—which is in the Ernaidhe of Dicuill. And two of the stones made of the cheese are there; the third one was, moreover, carried by Dicuill to Lughmagh when he was abbot there. It is to-day in Gort-Conaidh.

Sechnall asked something for the hymn. "As many as there are hairs in your *casula*," said Patrick, "if they are pupils of yours, and violate not rules, shall be saved. The clay of your abode has also been sanctified by God," said Patrick. "That will be received," said Sechnall. "Whosoever of the men of Eriu," said Patrick, "shall recite the three last chapters, or the three last lines, or the three last words, just before death, with pure mind, his soul will be saved." "*Deo gratias ago*," said Sechnall. Colman Ela recited it in his refectory thrice. Patrick stood in the middle of the house, when a certain plebeian asked, "Have we no other prayer that we could recite except this?" And Patrick went out afterwards. Cainnech, on the sea, in the south, saw the black cloud of devils passing over him. "Come here on your way," said Cainnech. The demons subsequently came, stating, "We went to meet the soul of a certain rich rustic observing the festival of Patrick; but his sons and people ate, and he sang two or three chapters of the hymn of Patrick; and, by your dignity, we thought it more a satire than praise of Patrick as they sang it; but by it we have been vanquished."

Part III

The miracles of Patrick are these—viz.: The hound in the territory of Gailenga, at Telach-Maine; the buck speaking out of the bodies of the thieves in the territory of Ui-Meith; the travelling of the garron without any guide to Druimmic-Ublae, when he lay down beside the grain of wheat; the chariot, without a charioteer, [going] from Armagh to Sleibhte; the appearance of the King of Britain in the form of a fox in his country, an ever-living miracle; a part of Aenach-Tailten, from which nothing dead is taken; the King of Cashel not to be killed by wounding, provided that he be of the race of Aenghus, son of Nadfraech; these bare residences not to lie demolished—viz., Rath-Airthir, and Sen-domhnach of Magh-Ai ("*Eccor Sen-domhnaigh*" is an old saying); Dun-Sobhairce charmed to the herenaghs—viz., an altar-sop with the Forbraige; and the *dominica* of Naas, and Magh-itir-da-glas in Macha; the navigation from Bertlach to Bertlach of Calry-Cuile-Cernadha; the streams which the *gilla* blessed at Drob-hais; the take [of fish] at Eastern Bann; the take at Sligo every quarter [of the year]; the Samer, which goes from the loughs of Erne to the sea—its eastern half, against Cenel-Conaill, is fruitful; its western part, towards Cenel-Cairbre, is unfruitful, through Patrick's word; Finn-glas, at the martyrhouse of Druim-Cain, and Druim-Cruachni; the taking of his kingship from Laeghaire, from Cairbre, from Fiacha, from Maine; the grant of his kingship to Eoghan, to Conall, to Crimthann, to Conall Erball; the smiths making the bells—*i.e.*, Mac Cecht, and Cuana, and Mac Tail; the artificers making the dishes and reliquaries and the altar chalices—viz., Tassach, and Essa, and Bitiu; the nuns making the altar-cloths—viz., Cochnass, and Tigris, and Lupait, and Darerca.

After these great miracles, however, the day of Patrick's death and of his going to heaven approached. What he began to do was to go to Armagh, that it might be there his resurrection would be. The angel Victor came to him. What he said to Patrick was: "It is not there thy resurrection has been decreed; go back to the place from whence you came (*i.e.*, to the Sabhall), for it is there God has decreed that you shall die—not in Macha. God has granted thee," said the angel, "that thy dignity and rule, thy devotion and teaching, shall be in Ard-Macha, as if thou thyself wert alive there."

The angel left advice with Patrick as to how he would be buried, saying: "Let two young, active oxen be brought," said he, "of the herds of Conall, from Finnabndir—*i.e.*, from Clochar; and let your body be placed in a wagon after them; and what way soever these young oxen go by themselves, and the place where they will stop, let it be there your interment shall be; and let there be a man's cubit in your

Tripartite Life of St. Patrick

grave, that your remains be not taken out of it." It was so done after his death. The oxen carried him to the place where to-day is Dun-da-leth-glas; and he was buried there with all honor and respect. And for a space of twelve nights—*i.e.*, whilst the divines were waking him with hymns and psalms and canticles—there was no night in Magh-inis, but angelic light there; and some say there was light in Magh-inis for the space of a year after Patrick's death, *quia nulli adanti viri meritum declarandum accidisse dubium est, et ita non visa nox in tota ilia regione in tempore luctus Patricii, qualiter Ezechiae langenti in horologio Achaz demonstrato sanitatis indicio, sol per XV lineas reversus est, et sic sol contra Gabon, et luna contra vallem Achilon stetit.*

In the first night the angels of the Lord of the elements were watching Patrick's body with spiritual chants. The fragrant odors of the divine grace which issued from the holy body, and the music of the angels, gave tranquillity and joy to the chief clerics of the men of Erin who were watching the body on the nights following; so that the blessing of Jacob to his son was kept regarding him—*i.e.*, *"Ecce odor filii mei sicut odor agri pleni, quem benedixit dicens,"* etc.

There was, moreover, a great attempt at conflict and battle between the provinces of Erin—viz., the Ulidians and the Ui-Neill and Airghialla—contending for Patrick's body. The Airghialla and Ui-Neill were trying to take it to Ard-Macha; the Ulidians were for keeping it with themselves. Then the Ui-Neill went to a certain water [river] there, when the river rose against them through the power of God. When the flood left the river, the hosts proceeded to quarrel—viz., the Ui-Neill and the Ulidians. It appeared then to each party of them that they were bringing the body to their own country, so that God separated them in this wise through the grace of Patrick.

The miracles so far shall be unto to-day. They are the miracles which the divines of Eriu heard, and which they put into order of narration. Colum-Cille, the son of Fedhlimidh, firstly, narrated and compiled the miracles of Patrick; Ultan, the descendant of Conchobhar; Adamnan, the grandson of Atinne; Eleran the wise; Ciaran of Belach-Duin; Bishop Ermedach of Clogher; Colman Uamach; and Cruimther Collaith of Druim-Roilgech.

A just man, indeed, was this man; with purity of nature like the patriarchs; a true pilgrim like Abraham; gentle and forgiving of heart like Moses; a praiseworthy psalmist like David; an emulator of wisdom like Solomon; a chosen vessel for proclaiming truth like the Apostle Paul. A man full of grace and of the knowledge of the Holy

Ghost like the beloved John. A fair flower-garden to children of grace; a fruitful vine-branch. A sparkling fire, with force of warmth and heat to the sons of life, for instituting and illustrating charity. A lion in strength and power; a dove in gentleness and humility. A serpent in wisdom and cunning to do good. Gentle, humble, merciful towards sons of life; dark, ungentle towards sons of death. A servant of labor and service of Christ. A king in dignity and power for binding and loosening, for liberating and convicting, for killing and giving life.

After these great miracles, therefore—*i.e.*, after resuscitating the dead; after healing lepers, and the blind, and the deaf, and the lame, and all diseases; after ordaining bishops, and priests, and deacons, and people of all orders in the Church; after teaching the men of Eriu, and after baptizing them; after founding churches and monasteries; after destroying idols and images and druidical arts—the hour of death of St. Patrick approached. He received the Body of Christ from the bishop, from Tassach, according to the advice of the angel Victor. He resigned his spirit afterwards to heaven, in the one hundred and twentieth year of his age. His body is here still in the earth, with honor and reverence. Though great his honor here, greater honor which will be to him in the Day of Judgment, when judgment will be given on the fruits of his teaching, like every great apostle, in the union of the apostles and disciples of Jesus; in the union of the nine orders of angels, which cannot be surpassed; in the union of the divinity and humanity of the Son of God; in the union which is higher than all unions—in the union of the Holy Trinity, Father, Son, and Holy Ghost. I beseech mercy through the intercession of Patrick. May we all arrive at that union; may we enjoy it for ever and ever. Amen.

These miracles, then, which we have related, the Lord performed for Patrick. Though one should attempt to recount them, he could not. Nevertheless, they are but a few of many related in commemoration; for there is no one who could remember them all. And there is no writer who could write all the prodigies and miracles he wrought in the countries he reached.

After the foundation, then, of numerous churches; after the consecration of monasteries; after baptizing the men of Eriu; after great abstinence and great labor; after destroying idols and images; after degrading numerous kings who would not obey him, and raising up those who obeyed him; and after he had three hundred and fifty or three hundred and seventy bishops; and after ordaining three thousand priests and persons of all other orders in the Church; after fasting and prayer; after showing mercy and mildness; after gentleness and sweetness towards sons of life; after the love of God and his neighbor, he received the body of Christ from the bishop, from Tassach; and he afterwards resigned his spirit to heaven. His body, lowever, is here on earth still, with honor and reverence. And though great his honor here, his honor will be greater in the Day of Judgment, when he will shine like a sun in heaven, and when judgment will be given regarding the fruit of his teaching, like Peter or Paul. He will be afterwards in the union of the patriarchs and prophets; in the union of the saints and virgins of the world; in the union of the apostles and disciples of Jesus Christ; in the union of the Church, both of heaven and earth; in the union of the nine orders of heaven, which cannot be surpassed; in the union of the divinity and humanity of the Son of God; in the union which excels every union—in the union of the Trinity, the Father, and the Son, and the Holy Ghost, for ever and ever. Amen. I beseech the mercy of God, through the intercession of Patrick. May we all reach that union; may we deserve it; may we inhabit it for ever and ever.

These are the four-and-twenty who were in orders with Patrick—viz., Sechnall, his bishop; Mochta, his priest; Bishop Ere, his brehon; Bishop MacCairthen, his strong man; Benen, his psalmist; Caemhan of Cill-Ruada, his youth; Sinell, from Cill-Daresis, his bell-ringer; Athgein of Both-Domhnach, his cook; Cruimther Mescan, from Domhnach-Mescan at Fochan, his brewer; Cruimther Bescna, from Domhnach-Dala, his mass-priest; Cruimther Catan and Cruimther Ocan, his two waiters; Odhran, from Disert-Odhran in Hy-Failghe, his charioteer; Cruimther Manach, his wood-man; Rodan, his shepherd; his three smiths, MacCecht, Laeban from Domhnach-Laebhan (who made the Findfaithnech), and Fortchern in Rath-Adiné. Essa and Bite and Tassach were his three artists. His three embroiderers were Lupait, and Ere, daughter of Daire, and Cruimthiris in Cenn-Gobha. And this is the number that were in the company of Joseph; and it is the number that is allowed at the table of the King of Cashel, down from the time of Fedhlimidh, son of Crimthann—*i.e.*, the king of the two provinces of Munster, etc.

The Annals of the Lord Jesus Christ, the year this Life of St. Patrick was written, 1477; and to-morrow will be Lammas Night. And in Baile-in-Miónín, in the house of O'Troightigh, this was written by Domhnall Albanach O'Troightigh; *et Deo gratias Jesu.*

Also from Benediction Books ...
Wandering Between Two Worlds: Essays on Faith and Art
Anita Mathias
Benediction Books, 2007
152 pages
ISBN: 0955373700

Available from www.amazon.com, www.amazon.co.uk

In these wide-ranging lyrical essays, Anita Mathias writes, in lush, lovely prose, of her naughty Catholic childhood in Jamshedpur, India; her large, eccentric family in Mangalore, a sea-coast town converted by the Portuguese in the sixteenth century; her rebellion and atheism as a teenager in her Himalayan boarding school, run by German missionary nuns, St. Mary's Convent, Nainital; and her abrupt religious conversion after which she entered Mother Teresa's convent in Calcutta as a novice. Later rich, elegant essays explore the dualities of her life as a writer, mother, and Christian in the United States-- Domesticity and Art, Writing and Prayer, and the experience of being "an alien and stranger" as an immigrant in America, sensing the need for roots.

About the Author

Anita Mathias was born in India, has a B.A. and M.A. in English from Somerville College, Oxford University and an M.A. in Creative Writing from the Ohio State University. Her essays have been published in The Washington Post, The London Magazine, The Virginia Quarterly Review, Commonweal, Notre Dame Magazine, America, The Christian Century, Religion Online, The Southwest Review, Contemporary Literary Criticism, New Letters, The Journal, and two of HarperSanFrancisco's The Best Spiritual Writing anthologies. Her non-fiction has won fellowships from The National Endowment for the Arts; The Minnesota State Arts Board; The Jerome Foundation, The Vermont Studio Center; The Virginia Centre for the Creative Arts, and the First Prize for the Best General Interest Article from the Catholic Press Association of the United States and Canada. Anita has taught Creative Writing at the College of William and Mary, and now lives and writes in Oxford, England.

www.anitamathias.com
wanderingbetweentwoworlds.blogspot.com (General and Culture)
thegoodbooksblog.blogspot.com (Reading and Writing)
theoxfordchristian.blogspot.com (Christian)